Food Storage
For The Health Of It

A Nutritional Guide
To Food Storage

Azrcka Bedgood

A to Z Nutrition
Powder Springs, GA

Published by: A to Z Nutrition
SAN 254-9980
Printed by: THP Printing, Conyers, Georgia
Edited by Debra Terry

Bedgood, Azrcka
Food Storage For The Health Of It / by Azrcka Bedgood
Includes bibliographical references
ISBN 0-9723824-0-2
1. Health 2. Nutrition
I. Title

This book is for educational purposes only and is not intended to be used for diagnosing or treatment of disease. Neither the publisher nor the author directly or indirectly dispense medical advice. This book does not claim to cure anything. This book presents research and nutritional information regarding grains, legumes, sprouts, and grasses that are in harmony with natural laws for good health and healing.

Dedication

This is dedicated to my Father In Heaven and his Son
Jesus Christ to whom I give all thanks, dedication
love and honor.

Special Acknowledgment

To my loving husband, Charles E Bedgood Sr. and to my
wonderful children, Rodney, Roger, Taunia, and Tricia
who supported me, gave me encouragement, and
helped with my every need.
A special thanks to Tarri, Falynn and Savannah for their
recipes and love.
To Tim, Sharron, Luanne, Sandra, Todd and Terry for
their confidence, and support.
And to my Parents Noell and Shirley Nelson with all my
Love.

Photos by Taunia Stein and Tricia Yother
Cover idea by my Father Noell Nelson
Cover Illustration by Tricia Yother

Table of Contents

Foreword

This book is for everyone interested in health and surviving these uncertain times. You will receive enough information to make your own choices when it comes to water purification, storage containers, and different grains. There is a list of grains that are the most compatible for babies, the elderly, or anyone with digestive problems. Included is a break down of vitamins, minerals, and amino acids of the grains and beans in this book.

There is a section on vitamins and minerals, and what major part of the body they effect. You will also be informed what nutrients help absorption of these vitamins and minerals, and some foods, drugs, and nutrients that inhibit the absorption.

You will become better informed why we as a nation are getting age related diseases at an earlier age and how we can take control of our health.

When you consume more whole grains, you and your family will become healthier and at the same time you will reduce your over all food bill. You have the choice to remain the same, or become more self-reliant, take control of your health, and feel more secure in the face of uncertainty.

Introduction to Food Storage
&
Why do we need to store Nutritional food?

With the state of the world and the threat of food contamination it is more important than ever that we store grain and know how to grow the live foods we need from the grains that we store. This book is meant to give you the information about these foods so you will have the desire to incorporate these foods into your diets now, not to have them sit on our shelves.

People are being caught up in the ways of the world and the fast food chains. The health crisis is upon us and we don't even recognize it.

According to the National Institute of Health:

- 1500 Americans die each day from cancer.
- 1 in 3 Americans will have cancer in their lifetime, it is expected to change to: 1 in 2.
- 1 in 8 women will be diagnosed with Breast cancer.
- 1.5 million Americans have heart attacks every year, 500,000 die.
- Heart attack causes more death and disability in Women than in Men and Women are more likely to die in the year after having a heart attack.
- 33 million Americans suffer from arthritis.
- 18% of Americans have hypertension.

What about our children?

- Cancer kills more children than any other disease, with more than 7,000 new cases every single year.
- 1 out of 2 children will develop heart disease.
- 1 in 4 children are obese.
- By the age of 12, children are already in the early stages of hardening of the arteries
- 7-10% of school age children has ADHD the National Institute of Health said it is primarily do to diet.

Deaths in the USA

- Over 65% of all deaths in the USA are caused by:
  Heart disease
  Cancer
  Stroke
- 70% of these deaths are due to diet.

It is time we became aware of these facts and begin to take charge of our health and our children's health. As parents we control for the most part the food that is brought into our homes and sat upon our tables. It is up to us to put the nourishing foods before the members of our household. It is up to them how much they eat.

This is where food storage comes in. For the most part it is far more economical to store nutritious whole foods, than processed foods. Gardening whether in the home, planter boxes, on the patio, or a full fledge garden brings us the fresh fruits and vegetables we need. Sprouting the grains we have will add additional fresh whole foods to our diet.

Food storage is like any other kind of preparations you

make. Preparing for winter you stock up on firewood, soups, hot cereals, etc. Summer you plan for outdoor fun, lightweight clothing, quick sandwiches, etc. Vacations you plan what you'll need, what you have, and what you need to get in order to have a successful fun filled low stress event.

Food storage is all about, providing high quality, highly nutritious foods to sustain us for a particular period-of-time (everyday). You should aim for a year supply of food. Now a year supply of food may seem overwhelming, when you think of all the trips you make to the store in one month. And where will you put all that food. You will be changing (hopefully) your life style. Grains can store in a small amount of space compared to pre-packaged processed foods that have very little useable nutrients.

You will find when storing and **using** grains, beans, etc. in your diet you will be spending less money on your food bill and your family will become much healthier. That sounds like a good trade off to me. After all if we have our health (and we can have better health by eating more whole grains), we can deal with life's unexpected situations in a better frame of mind.

I am going to emphasize the nutrients of the different grains, discuss some vitamins, minerals, amino acids, protein, etc. what functions of the body they are good for and some of the effects on the body when deficient in these nutrients. Some nutrients can be completely depleted from your body's storehouse over five years before you will see any side affects. It is because the body has the ability to extract nutrients from other areas of the body to maintain balance as best it can in spite of ourselves. This however cannot last forever. We will eventually show or feel signs of disease.

The dietary sources listed are not listed in any particular order they do not necessarily indicate the highest to lowest quantity of each particular nutrient. These nutrients are not miracle cures; they are miracle nutrients that sustain our bodies. Everyone is deficient in some nutrients. This is why we have billion dollar companies selling us drugs, vitamins, minerals, protein, herbs, amino acids, etc. Some are synthetic, natural, organic, and inorganic or "non-organic", chelated, some combine vitamins and minerals, and some are single nutrients. These are not all bad. Most of our needs for these packaged nutrients come about from the fast food society we live in, and the neglect or abuse we have shown our bodies.

Food storage is not a gloom and doom project. Food storage can be a fun project and when completed, or even partially completed you will have great satisfaction in a job well done. In planning the foods to be stored by your family (and all families are different) you can take time to look at the quality, quantity, and food value of the items you will store. First things first, you may have more or less than you think. Take inventory of what you have on hand. With the foods in your home, could you sustain your life and your family's life for a week, a month, six months, a year, or more? Many circumstances could be made much easier if you had additional food stored.

There are several methods of building up your food supply and becoming more secure and self-reliant. You will need to be consistent in your efforts to build up your supplies.

Water next to the air we breath, is the most important item to store, and the least likely item to be on the top of your list. It would be wise to have a two-week supply of water on hand. This means one gallon a day per person for an emergency.

It would be impossible to store a one-year supply of water. You should strive for at least a two-week supply of water for each person. Emergency water for two weeks would be 14 gallons per person.

You can sustain life for one person for a year, if you have the following items: Wheat and other grains 400 pounds. Legumes (include dry beans, split peas, lentils, etc.) 60 pounds. Powdered Milk 16 to 20 pounds, or (extra soybeans or sweet brown rice to make up the difference). Honey sixty to one hundred pounds and or sweeteners equivalent to that. Salt 8 to 10 pounds. Oil 2 to 6 six gallons. Vitamin C (ascorbic Acid) a minimum 500 to 1000 mg daily.

Let's face it. This would be a drastic adjustment to most of our life styles if we had to adjust to just sustaining life, but sustain our family's life we must. It is our duty to take care of our families. It is not the responsibility of Government, Church, or neighbors to take care of our needs. We as a society have become so accustomed to all the abundance and fast foods this great land has provided for us for so long. We would scarcely know what to do, if we had to rely on the grains and food products that we should have in our homes.

Once you have your grains, beans, rice, honey, and other necessities and learn to prepare these foods, learn to sprout some of your grains and to juice your wheat and barley grasses. You and your family will become much healthier.

In the ever changing times that we are living in. A false sense of security exists in this world today. The only real security we have is God and the talents he has given to each one of us. For us to become more self-reliant is just good common sense.

In this book I have listed some of the nutrient values for some grains, beans, and sweeteners. These tables were obtained from the USDA and can be found on the Internet at: http://www.nal.usda.gov/fnic/foodcomp

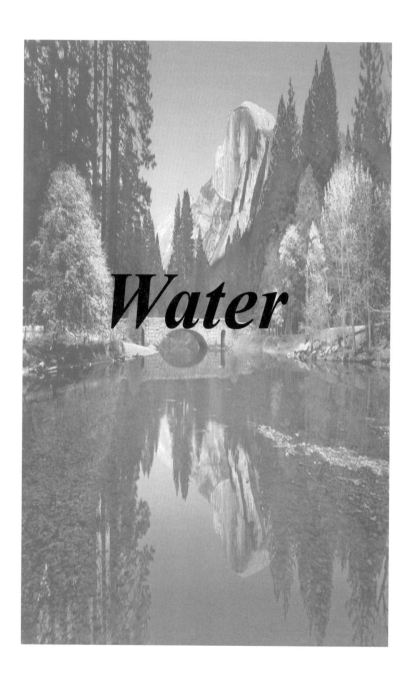

Water

 Water is probably the cheapest preparedness item to acquire. Water is the easiest to store, weighs the most, and takes up more space. Without clean water we cannot experience optimum health. Water is essential to all life. A person can live weeks without food, but only days without water. Having an ample supply of clean water is top priority in an emergency and in your long-term storage program. Water is so important to human survival; experts say you should never ration it. Drink at least 2.6 quarts per day, as long as supplies last, and look for alternative water sources.

Experts differ on the amount of water they tell us to drink each day. Some say at least eight, 8 ounce glasses of water per day. Others go by body weight for adults and say ½ ounce of water per one pound of body weight per day. Still others say drink when you are thirsty, again others say by the time you are thirsty you are dehydrated.

Regardless of the formula you use, we can not survive without water. Everyone should store the minimum water requirement for his or her family's emergency needs. You should store enough water for two weeks. The rule of thumb is one gallon per day per person. This will depend on the needs of your family; you will need more if you live in a hot climate, for young children, if someone is ill, and for nursing mothers. The very minimum is fourteen gallons per person per week. This does not include water for sanitary purposes, bathing, etc.

Water is an unappreciated resource until there's a crisis. Wouldn't it be better to spend a few minutes now, rather than hours later looking to find or buy water for you and your loved ones? Storing water can be as easy as turning on your faucet, if you store it before an emergency arises.

Good water storage containers are heavy enough to hold water, airtight, and breakage resistant. They should stack well and have a lining that won't rust or affect the flavor of the water.

 Depending on your storage area you can store your water in a one-gallon, five gallon, eight gallon, fifteen gallon, thirty gallon, or in fifty-five gallon drums. These should be food-grade drums. If you have limited storage space, shipping-grade water containers, when filled with water are capable of withstanding most temperatures outdoors both hot and cold. This is very important if some of your volume of water must be stored outside the pro-tected area of your home, or if you live in an area where rodents are a common problem.

Do not use the excuse that you don't have the "proper" container to store some water. You can use clean sterilized Soda bottles. Sterilized glass canning jars or bottles will store water well; the drawback is they can break.

The only bleach bottles that should be used to store water, are the ones that only contain the 5.25% to 6% sodium hypochlorite (IT SHOULD NOT BE USED AS DRINKING WATER BECAUSE THE CHEMICALS USED IN THE PLASTIC ARE NOT FOOD GRADE, THIS WATER CAN BE FOR OTHER USES). The other bleach bottles have been contaminated with other additives and should not be used at all. Plastic milk bottles should not be use for long storage for they are made to break down.

If your water is free of bacteria and if you keep it in a clean, tightly closed container, filled to the top with no air space, away from sunlight, it will remain safe almost indefinitely. To purify your water before storing it, add any brand household bleach that contains 5.25% to 6% sodium hypochlorite only. This is becoming harder to find, do not use bleach that has been scented, thickened, color safe, or has any other inert ingredients in it. Your water will not be safe to use as drinking water.

To pre-clean or disinfect your containers:

Flush containers to remove any sediment or particles if necessary.
Disinfect a five-gallon container by filling it half full of water then add 1/4 cup of bleach. Mix and then fill up the rest of the container with water. For larger containers increase the amount of water and bleach for rinsing.
Drain the solution from the container and flush thoroughly with fresh water to remove the solution.
Fill the container half full with fresh water.
Add 10 drops of bleach per gallon container.

Fill the container to the top, leaving no air space between the top and the cap.
Make sure the caps are on good and tight to prevent the air from getting into the container. This prevents the bleach from dissipating.
Store the containers in a cool dark area.

Indoor Water Supplies

 After a disaster, it is possible that the water supply could be cut off from your home or it may become contaminated. Your main source of water in your home will be from your hot water heater, the toilet tanks if chemicals have not been added, and water pipes in your home. First turn off the water supply to your home. This will eliminate contaminated water from coming in. There is an air release connected to the water heater that will allow you to drain the water from the water heater when needed. To drain water from the pipes turn on the faucet at the highest point which releases the air pressure and allows you to drain the water from the lowest faucet.

Avoid water from waterbeds for drinking water. Chemicals are in the plastic casing of the bed and additional chemicals have probably been added to the water to prevent the growth of algae, fungi, and bacteria. The water from the waterbed can be used to laundry clothes, flush toilets; it takes approx. 2 ½ gallons to flush a toilet, etc.

Outside Water Supplies

Rain water, streams, rivers, and other moving bodies of water (DO NOT DRINK FLOOD WATER), ponds and lakes, natural springs, swimming pools, hot tubs and water in the coiled garden hose can be used after it has been purified.

Avoid water with floating material, an odor or dark color. Use salt water only if you distill it first. Again remember do not ration water. Drink the amount you need today, and find more tomorrow. You can minimize the amount of water your body needs by reducing activity and staying cool.

Water that has been contaminated with toxic chemicals or radioactive materials may not be purified successfully using home decontamination methods.

Purifying water

Any water that is obtained from sources outside the home or water that does not appear clear should be sterilized. Whatever method you choose to use, make sure you have at least two methods on hand to purify your water.

Chlorine
To purify water with bleach you must use bleach that contains 5.25% to 6% sodium hypochlorite only; no other inert ingredients for it will not be safe for drinking. Add 7 to 10 drops of bleach per gallon of clear water, depending on the strength, and 14 to 20 drops of bleach if the water is

cloudy. Stir or shake well. Let the water stand for 30 minutes. The water should have a distinct taste or smell of chlorine, if it doesn't then repeat the dosage and wait another 15 minutes. If you still cannot smell or taste the chlorine discard the water. The detection of chlorine in the water is a sign of safety. Chlorine can become weak with age or for other reasons.

Chlorine is used to disinfect the water and make it safe to drink. It is the simplest and least expensive method, yet it has its drawbacks. Chlorine is not as effective against the hard-shelled protozoa such as Giardia and Cryptosporidium. Most people don't like the taste or the smell, and chlorine is a chemical contaminant that some people may have reactions to.

Chlorine can be remove from the water by a solid carbon block filter, reverse osmosis, or distilling the water.

Iodine
The newer iodine-bases tablets will store about three years. Water treated with iodine may still look and smell bad. You may need a waiting period in order for the chemical to kill harmful microorganisms.

Boiling
Boiling is one methods of purifying water. Most disease causing microorganisms cannot survive the intense heat. At sea level bring water to a rolling boil for 1 minute to kill bacteria and parasites; boil 10 minutes to destroy viruses. Add 1 minute for every 1,000 feet of elevation. In the mountains at 10,000 feet water must be boiled for 10-20 minutes, depending on your concerns. Let the water cool.

Gently pour the water into another container for drinking. Leave about ½ inch of water in the bottom of the pan. This can be put into another container for washing or other needs. All the dead microorganisms, minerals and contaminants will settle to the bottom of the water. It will not necessarily hurt you, but I prefer to use it for other needs. Now that you are ready to drink the water, shake it or pour it back and forth between clean containers to put oxygen back in the water, this makes for better tasting water.

While these two methods of chemical or boiling water will kill most microorganisms in water, distilling water will remove microorganisms that resist these methods, heavy metals, salts, and most other chemicals.

Distilling

There are several small distillers on the market, or you can create a method to distill your own water. Salt water can be distilled and used for drinking. Distilling is just boiling the water and catching the steam. Once the stem has cooled, it will condense into droplets of water that are captured for drinking. The condensed vapor will not contain salt and other impurities. Keep in mind when boiling water and distilling your own water (without a commercial distiller) you will loose some water to evaporation.

Portable Water Filters

There are portable filter units designed for biking, travel, or camping. These are small units designed to use lake or spring water. Depending on the unit they will remove some chemicals and microorganism.

Charcoal

In an emergency if you are unsure of the water and don't have a way to purify it; you can use charcoal to absorb impurities in the water. You can buy charcoal, or if you are out in the wild you can scrape the charcoal from a burnt log. Do not use ashes it has to be the black charcoal. Filter the water first through a clean cloth or cotton shirt if possible. You would fill a container ¼ of the way full of the fine charcoal. Then add the strained clear water. You would shake well and then drink the charcoal and water mixture. Charcoal is used in many water filters; it is also used internally to absorb many poisons that a person might swallow.

Nutrition

Nutrients

This section allows you to see the importance of whole grains, legumes, sprouting, juicing, fresh fruits and vegetables. How vital their nutrients are to our health and mental wellbeing. These grains were created for our use not for our misuse of refining and depleting the nutrients that we so desperately need to maintain an optimal body. This section was not meant for diagnosing, but rather to let you see if we were to use grains, legumes, fruits, and vegetables as the majority of our food intake we could avoid all together or at least lessen the possibility of disease in our bodies.

In this section I have listed some vitamins and minerals along with a few of their functions, some of the food sources, some items that inhibits absorption of vitamins and minerals, some nutrients that enhances absorption, and just some of the deficiency symptoms that can occur. The food sources are not listed in any particular order of nutrients. Although I have listed the grasses first because they are a more complete food source than any other food and the easiest to assimilate when juiced.

Note: *This section is not a complete listing of the above items, for each nutrient could have a whole book written about the intricate functions they play in our bodies. The general deficiency symptoms referred to can occur when the daily intake of the vitamins or minerals has been less than our bodies need to function properly over a prolonged period. These nonspecific symptoms do not alone prove nutritional deficiency. They may be caused by any* *number of conditions or may have functional causes. If these symptoms persist, they may indicate a condition other than a vitamin or mineral deficiency; you may want to consult your medical practitioner.*

It is important to be healthy and regain the nutrients that have been lost in our bodies by consuming so many processed foods. The fact is pure whole foods are the best thing for your body. Whole foods give your body what it needs to heal itself. In whole foods the vitamins, minerals, and amino acids are in balanced proportion for our bodies to assimilate the nutrients. For example you need magnesium to assimilate calcium properly, in whole food you will find this combination. Vitamin E needs selenium for your body to absorb it properly. All of the whole foods are created with you in mind. The nutrients in Whole foods complement each other; variety is the key to balanced nutrition.

More and more people have become wheat intolerant. This is usually because of the state in which the body is in. There is also Spelt which is an ancient wheat that most wheat sensitive people can tolerate well. Kamut is also a wheat that has been used with great success. Triticale is a grain that has been genetically crossed between wheat and rye. The kernels are larger than wheat. It is said it has a higher protein efficiency rate than wheat, and a higher percentage of protein.

Wheat grass juice is essential in moving our bodies towards a more alkaline state, thus creating better health. In this state the body has the optimum ability to heal its self.

Wheatgrass is a superior source of chlorophyll and has the widest range of minerals and vitamins. It contains all of the vitamins and most of the minerals needed for optimum maintenance and well being. Wheatgrass juice resembles the molecular structure of hemin. Heim is part of hemoglobin, which is the vital part of our blood that carries the oxygen throughout our body. The difference is Wheatgrass juice is magnesium based and hemoglobin is iron based. Wheatgrass juice is a red blood cell builder, stimulator, and rejuvenator. It helps to cleanse the liver, kidneys, and urinary tract as it purifies the blood. There has been identified over 80 different enzymes in "Grass" and it contains approximately 30 different enzymes crucial to our bodies. Chlorophyll also has the ability to break down poisonous carbon dioxide and release free oxygen.

Grasses of Wheat (red hard winter wheat is the best wheat for growing grass for juicing), Barley, Rye and Oats grasses are also excellent sources of vitamins, minerals, amino acids, enzymes, and fatty acids.

Barleygrass is high in organic sodium. Organic sodium keeps calcium in solution in the bloodstream and is known to dissolves calcium deposited on the joints. It replenishes the organic sodium in the lining of the stomach. This aids digestion by improving the production of hydrochloric acid in the stomach. Barleygrass juice is also loaded with vitamins, minerals, and enzymes along with chlorophyll.

When wheat and barley are sprouted and grown into grass; then juiced, all the nutrients are assimilated easily by the body. Wheatgrass juice is very sweet, and barley grass juice is bitter tasting compared to wheatgrass.

When storing and using grains and legumes I store organic foods. Most foods you can find grown organically. If you are going to store only for a time of crisis doesn't it make sense to store the purest foods available? Why add another burden to your body. If you have health problems why would you want to add pesticides, preservatives, artificial colors, additives and other chemicals to your body. Your lungs, heart, kidneys, liver, pancreas, and colon do not need or want the added stress of trying to eliminate all these toxins.

Listed are just some of the minerals, vitamins, and amino acids to assist you in choosing the grains, legumes, seeds, and other nutritional items for your home storage.

Protein

Protein

Protein is the basis of all life. All body tissues depend on protein in some way. Wounds won't heal if your body does not have enough protein. I have seen in a hospital when a person is protein deficient the incision wouldn't heal. When a protein substance was given by internal feeding in a matter of days you could see new tissue growth. Protein is not made within the body and needs to be supplied every day to maintain good health. Your body can store protein, but not for long.

Experts say that Americans eat too much protein for good health. Experts disagree on the percent of protein needed it ranges from 2.5% to 10% of your total daily calories. A 2,000-caloric diet allows for approx. 50 grams of protein. The average protein consumed by Americans is approx. 90 grams per day. The National Academy of Science now recommends that Americans reduce their protein intake by 12 to 15 percent and switch from animal to plant protein sources.

Protein does not burn cleanly, leaving nitrogen waste thereby straining your kidneys, which is linked to urinary tract infections. For people who are diabetics this extra workload increases the risk of serious kidney disease. In digesting protein our body must increase its metabolic rate by 10%, which also puts a strain on the livers ability to absorb oxygen.

Most of us do not digest all the protein taken into our bodies. This can cause what is called sticky blood, which can affect many functions of the body. What we need are natural enzymes to help us digest these proteins. We find these enzymes in fresh fruits, vegetables, sprouts, and juiced grasses.

Dietary protein supplies essential amino acids and nitrogen for the synthesis of enzymes, hormones, and other internal body proteins.

We can have access to these live enzymes every day by sprouting our grains and legumes. Sprouting takes very little space; as little as a glass jar. Everyone can sprout grains or legumes; a variety can be put in the same jar.

Dietary Sources: Grasses of Wheat, Barley, Rye, and Oats juiced, Whole grain wheat, millet, barley, rye, buckwheat, amaranth, quinoa, spelt, kamut, and oats. Legumes, soy beans, nuts, seeds, and meats.

Minerals

Minerals

Minerals are used in almost every function of the body and are essential for our basic life processes and good health. They are necessary to activate many of the vitamins our body must have to function properly. Most of us do not get enough minerals into our systems either because the body cannot accept the minerals in the form we are receiving them, for example inorganic minerals, or because of poor digestion.

The first thing our bodies must do is to dissolve the minerals. Second the body wraps the minerals in a molecule of protein, this is called chelation (pronounced key - lation). This is essential since the blood stream will not accept a mineral until it has been chelated. If the minerals are not accepted by the body to activate vitamins, both the vitamin and the mineral will pass from our system with no benefit.

Minerals are not produced in the body and must be derived from our food source. We assimilate minerals best from plants rather than animal sources. Plants are able to absorb the minerals and convert them in a way that our bodies are better able to utilize them. If some minerals are depleted from the soil, the plants cannot provide us with something that is not there. We must give back to the earth that which has been taken.

Calcium

Calcium is the most abundant mineral in our bodies. Calcium works with phosphorus in the development of normal bones and teeth; assists blood clotting, maintains nerve transmission, and works with magnesium for cardio-vascular health and in maintaining heart rhythm, and nerve conduction. Every living cell needs calcium. With high phosphorus to calcium ratio 4:1 or 5:1 excess calcium is removed from bone and eliminated, which causes bone demineralization. Kidney stone forming people need calcium citrate, it increases urinary citrate that inhibits formation of calcium stones. Estrogen levels effect calcium, there can be rapid loss of calcium after menopause due to lower estrogen levels. Calcium must have sufficient vitamin D to be absorbed by the body.

We constantly lose calcium from our bloodstream through urine, sweat, and feces. It is renewed with calcium from our bones. In this process, bones continuously lose calcium. This bone calcium must be replaced from food.

How rapidly calcium is lost depends, in part, on the kind and amount of protein you eat as well as other diet and lifestyle choices. Diets high in protein cause more calcium to be lost through the urine. Protein from animal products is much more likely to cause calcium loss than protein from plant foods.

> **Dietary Sources:** Kamut, Wheat Grass juice, Barley Grass juice, Leafy green vegetables, Pinto beans, Adzuki beans, Tofu, Molasses, Black beans, Great

northern beans, Kidney beans, Soybeans, Mung beans, Flaxseed, Almonds, Alfalfa sprouts, Apples, Grapefruits, and Broccoli. All grains have some calcium, but Amaranth has far more calcium than all the other grains.

Inhibits Absorption: Stress, Lack of Hydrochloric acid, Lack of exercise, Lack of magnesium, Lack of Vitamin D, Diuretic drugs (Loop Diuretics) and Hormone drug (Corticosteroids). In high phosphorus to calcium ratios excess calcium is removed from bone and eliminated, which causes bone demineralization. Alcohol inhibits calcium absorption. Caffeine increases the rate at which calcium is lost through urine. The mineral boron may slow the loss of calcium from bones.

Enhances Absorption: Magnesium, Hydrochloric acid, Vitamins A, D, C, F, and Iron. Vitamin D is needed for absorption of calcium and phosphorus from the digestive tract, and helps in maintaining normal blood calcium levels.

Deficiency Symptoms: Back and leg pain, Heart palpitations, Brittle bones, Insomnia, Tooth decay, and Muscle pain. Bone problems can occur with prolonged calcium deficiency. Poor growth, Muscle and nerve irritability, Painful joints, and Cataracts.

Iron

Iron is needed for formation of hemoglobin. Iron is the central core of the hemoglobin molecule. Iron combines with proteins and copper to produce hemoglobin, which carries oxygen throughout the body. Calcium, cooper, cobalt, and vitamin C need to be present in order for iron to do its work. Iron promotes protein metabolism and good healthy teeth, skin, nails, and bones. However, free, unbound iron can be toxic at high levels (commercial supplements). If extra Iron is needed, use a food source iron to avoid this situation. Women should not be taking iron supplements only in the case of anemia and directed by a medical practitioner, and only until the condition has been corrected.

Dietary Sources: Wheatgrass juice, Barleygrass juice, Kamutgrass juice, Ryegrass juice, Oatgrass juice, Molasses, Raisins, Apricots, Prunes, Leafy green vegetables, Broccoli, Spinach, Peas, Beet-greens, Endive, Cherry juice, Blackstrap Molasses, Whole wheat, Millet, Oats, Brown rice, Wheat germ, Dried fruits, Beans and Dried peas; Soy-beans, Kidney beans, Lima beans, Whole Grains, Almonds, Brazil nuts, Sunflower seeds, and most Seeds. White meat Chicken, Dark meat Turkey.

Inhibits Absorption: Excessive zinc (other than food sources), Coffee and Tea contain tannin, a substance that if drank with meals can cut iron absorption by 40-95%. Excessive phosphorus (other than natural food sources). Iron is blocked by phosphates these are added to ice cream, candy bars, baked-goods, beer and soft drinks. EDTA, an additive in many canned and processed foods inhibit iron absorption.

Enhances Absorption: Copper, Vitamins C, B-12, Folic acid, Calcium, Vinegar, Citrus juice, Alfalfa, and Watercress.

Deficiency Symptoms: Weakness, difficulty in breathing, anemia, constipation and brittle nails. Un-bound iron can be toxic at abnormally high levels. Iron overload is linked to some cancers, heart disease, diabetes, arthritis, and glandular malfunctions. Using herbal or food source iron avoids these problems.

Magnesium

Magnesium is a catalyst in the utilization of carbohydrates, fats, protein, phosphorus, calcium, and potassium. Magnesium is a critical mineral for osteoporosis and skeletal structure. Magnesium is necessary for good nerve and muscle function. It also helps in maintaining energy, healthy bones, arteries, heart, nerves, and teeth. Magnesium also helps calm hyperactive children and is considered the "antistress" mineral. Magnesium is believed necessary for production of the brain chemical serotonin.

Dietary Sources: Wheatgrass juice, Barleygrass juice, Kamutgrass juice, Ryegrass juice, Oatgrass juice, Lima beans, Navy beans, Molasses, Whole grains, Millet, Brown rice, Honey, Nuts especially: Almonds, Pecans, Cashews, and Brazil nuts, Seeds, Bran, Dark green vegetables, Beans, Hot spices, Avocado and dried Apricots.

Inhibits Absorption: Diuretic drugs (Loop Diuretics), Hormone drug (Estrogen) and Anti-rheumatic drug (Penicillamine).

Enhances Absorption: Vitamins B-6, C, D, Protein, and Calcium.

Deficiency Symptoms: Muscle spasms, Stomach disturbances, Confusion, Fatigue, Nervousness, Decreased learning ability, and Poor memory. Magnesium deficiency can play a role in some mental disorders.

Phosphorus

Phosphorus is the second most abundant element in the body. It's Necessary for skeletal structure, brain oxygenation and cell reproduction. Phosphorus works with calcium to form bones and teeth. It is also necessary for cell growth and repair. Phosphorus utilizes carbohydrate, fat, and protein. It also helps with the contractions of the heart muscle, and nerve activity. The ideal ratio of calcium to phosphorus in the diet should be equal. Most red meats and poultry have much more phosphorus than calcium. Phosphorus is added to soft drinks in high amounts. At this time calcium is not being added to soft drinks, therefore the imbalance causes calcium to be removed from the bones and eliminated, which can cause bone demineralization.

Dietary Sources: Wheatgrass juice, Barleygrass juice, Kamutgrass juice, Ryegrass juice, Oatgrass juice, Beans, Nuts, Bone meal.

Inhibits Absorption: Excessive intake of Iron, Magnesium (other than food source), and White sugar.

Enhances Absorption: Protein, Manganese, Iron, Calcium, Vitamins A, F, and D.

Deficiency Symptoms: Appetite loss, Irregular breathing, Fatigue, and Nervousness.

Potassium

Potassium is one of the main blood minerals called "electrolytes". Potassium helps in the balance of acid-alkaline in the system, transmitting electrical signals between cells, and nerves. Potassium controls the activity of the heart muscles, nervous system, and kidneys. Potassium helps oxygenate the brain for clear thinking. A diet high in fruits, vegetables, and whole grain is rich in potassium and low in sodium, which helps to maintain normal blood pressure.

> **Dietary Sources:** Wheatgrass juice, Barleygrass juice, Kamutgrass juice, Ryegrass juice, Oatgrass juice, Whole grains, Seeds, Beans, Dried fruits, Dates, Figs, Raisins, Peaches, Nuts, Bananas, Apricots, Kiwis, Strawberries, Potatoes, Spinach, Lettuce, Parsley, Ginger, Spices like Basil, Cumin, Coriander, Hot peppers, Dill weed, Tarragon, Paprika, and Turmeric.
>
> **Inhibits Absorption:** Coffee, Diuretics, White sugar, Stress, Alcohol, Cortisone, Laxatives. (People who take high blood pressure medication are vulnerable to potassium deficiency), and Diuretic drugs (Loop Diuretics).
>
> **Enhances Absorption:** Vitamin B-6, and Sodium
>
> **Deficiency Symptoms:** Respiratory failure, cardiac arrest, poor reflexes, dry skin, irregular heartbeat (slow), insomnia, Fatigue, Muscle weakness.

Sodium

Sodium is an electrolyte mineral that helps regulate kidney and body fluid functions. Sodium is related to high blood pressure only when calcium and phosphorous are deficient in the body. Sodium acts as an anti-dehydrating agent. High blood pressure is becoming an epidemic in our country. When natural foods are the only source of sodium, there is almost no hypertension.

>**Dietary Sources:** Almost all foods contain some sodium, particularly as sodium chloride. Good food sources: Wheatgrass juice, Barleygrass juice, Kamutgrass juice, Ryegrass juice, Oatgrass juice, Celery, Whole grains, Beans, Beets, Carrots, Kelp and Artichokes. No wholesome natural food has a high salt content.

>**Inhibits Absorption:** Unknown

>**Enhances Absorption:** Calcium and Phosphorous.

>**Deficiency Symptoms:** Usually associated with excessive water loss, nausea, vomiting, dizziness, poor memory, and muscle weakness. More serious, circulatory collapse and shock may occur.

Zinc

Zinc is essential to the formation of insulin, and immune strength. Zinc helps prevent birth defects, and accelerates healing. Zinc also aids in the digestion and metabolism of phosphorus, protein, and carbohydrates. As is the saying "Think Zinc", it is a brain food and helps with mental alertness. Zinc also helps fight free radical damage. A high stress lifestyle depletes zinc, impairing immune response and the ability to heal. Zinc also helps detoxify alcohol from the liver.

Dietary Sources: Wheatgrass juice, Barleygrass juice, Kamutgrass juice, Ryegrass juice, Oatgrass juice, Brewer's yeast, Soybeans, Spinach, Wheat germ, Mushrooms, Whole Wheat, Rye, Oats, Sunflower, Pumpkin and Caraway seeds, Brazil nuts, Ginger root, Mustard, and Chili powder.

Inhibits Absorption: Alcohol and a high in take of Calcium (other than food source), Anti-rheumatic drug (Penicillamine), and Diuretic drugs (Loop Diuretics).

Enhances Absorption: Phosphorus, Copper, and Vitamin A.

Deficiency Symptoms: Sterility, Loss of taste, Poor appetite, Fatigue, and Retarded growth.

Copper

Copper aids in the production of red blood cells, and assists in enzyme functions. Copper is needed for iron absorption and for bone formation. Copper is part of many enzymes. SOD (superoxide dismutase) is a copper-containing enzyme that protects against free radical damage. Copper also helps control inflammation.

> **Dietary Sources:** Wheatgrass juice, Barleygrass juice, Kamutgrass juice, Ryegrass juice, Oatgrass juice, Soybeans, Raisins, Nuts, Beans, and Molasses.

> **Inhibits Absorption:** High intakes of Zinc (other than food source) and Anti-rheumatic drug (Penicillamine).

> **Enhances Absorption:** Zinc, Cobalt, and Iron.

> **Deficiency Symptoms:** Skin sores, Impaired respiration, General weakness, High cholesterol, Anemia, and heart arrhythmia. Excess copper can result in mental depression.

Manganese

Manganese nourishes the brain and nerve centers. It is also important in digesting proteins. Manganese helps in enzyme activation and its immune enhancing activity. Manganese is needed for normal skeletal development; it also helps in the utilization of vitamin E.

Dietary Sources: Wheatgrass juice, Barleygrass juice, Kamutgrass juice, Ryegrass juice, Oatgrass juice, Whole grains, Nuts, Legumes, Bananas, Green vegetables, Celery, Pineapple, Egg yolks, Ginger, Blueberries, and Rice.

Inhibits Absorption: Excessive consumption of phosphorus and calcium (other than food source). Tranquilizer drugs deplete manganese.

Enhances Absorption: Phosphorus, Calcium, Vitamins B-1, and E.

Deficiency Symptoms: Hearing loss, dizziness, poor hair and nail growth (white spots on nails), and poor muscle-joint coordination.

Selenium

Selenium is a necessary part of a powerful antioxidant enzyme; it helps protect the body from free radical damage. It also seems to help protect us against heavy metal toxicity. It works with Vitamin E to prevent cholesterol build up. Selenium works with vitamin E to help preserve tissue elasticity and helps prevent degenerative diseases. Good Selenium levels correlate with low cancer rates. In order to make sure we get the selenium we need we must eat a variety of wholesome foods.

> **Dietary Sources:** Wheatgrass juice, Barleygrass juice, Kamutgrass juice, Ryegrass juice, Oatgrass juice, Whole grains, Wheat germ, Brewer's yeast, Bran, Sesame seeds, Garlic, Molasses, Nuts, Brazil nuts, Barley, Oats, Brown rice, Broccoli, Onions, Tomatoes, Radishes, Lamb and Salmon.

> **Inhibits Absorption:** Unknown.

> **Enhances Absorption:** Vitamin E.

> **Deficiency Symptoms:** Premature aging, liver damage, hypothyroidism and possible cancer of the digestive tract.

Vitamins

Vitamin C

Vitamin C is a strong antioxidant. Vitamin C helps promote healthy teeth, gums, bones, and strengthens blood vessels. It also helps increases absorption of iron. Vitamin C accelerates healing and helps with the production of and maintenance of collagen tissue. Vitamin C also helps in controlling alcohol craving. Vitamin C helps in resisting infection and over all health. Without adequate vitamin C bones can not utilize calcium. Diabetics need more vitamin C, when blood sugar rises to high levels it competes with vitamin C for entry into the cells. The higher the blood sugar level the less vitamin C enters the cells. This lack of vitamin C absorption seems to be one reason Diabetics heal slower.

Dietary Sources: Wheatgrass juice, Barleygrass juice, Kamutgrass juice, Ryegrass juice, Oatgrass juice, Sprouted Wheat, Barley, and Alfalfa seeds, Wheat and Barley grass, Tomatoes, Peppers, Citrus Fruits, Papaya, Cantaloupe, Broccoli, and Strawberries.

Inhibits Absorption: Stress, High fever, Tobacco, Antibiotics, Aspirin, Cortisone, Oral contraceptives, and Tetracycline, and High blood sugar levels.

Enhances Absorption: Bioflavonoids, Calcium, Magnesium, Most vitamins and minerals.

Deficiency Symptoms: Muscular weakness, anemia, appetite loss, skin hemorrhages, swollen joints, slow healing wounds and fractures, bleeding gums, easy bruising, low resistance to infections.

Thiamine - Vitamin B-1

Vitamin B-1 is known for its benefits for calming nerves and mental attitude. Vitamin B-1 helps in maintaining healthy skin, mouth, eyes, hair, and stabilizes appetite. It is necessary for carbohydrate metabolism. Vitamin B-1 is essential for normal functioning of the heart, nerve-tissues, muscles, digestion, learning capacity, and promotes proper growth in children. Vitamin B-1 also enhances immune response and helps control motion sickness.

Dietary Sources: Wheatgrass juice, Barleygrass juice, Kamutgrass juice, Ryegrass juice, Oatgrass juice, Whole wheat, Whole grains, Wheat germ, Brown rice, Legumes, Nuts, Brewer's yeast, Asparagus, Seeds, and Soy foods.

Inhibits Absorption: Tobacco, Coffee, Alcohol, Stress, Fever, Sugar, Raw clams, and Heavy metal pollutants. Pregnancy, lactation, diuretics, and oral contraceptives require extra thiamine.

Enhances Absorption: Sulfur, Manganese, Niacin, Vitamins B-2, C, E, B Complex, and Folic acid.

Deficiency Symptoms: Depression, constipation, impaired growth in children, shortness of breath, numbness of hands and feet, sensitivity to noise, loss of appetite, poor memory and poor muscle coordination, heart damage, and weight loss.

Riboflavin - Vitamin B-2

Vitamin B-2 is use for energy production, and for fat and carbohydrate metabolism. Vitamin B-2 is also necessary for antibody and red blood cell formation. Riboflavin promotes good healthy eyes, hair, skin, and nails, and it also helps to prevent cataracts. Vitamin B-2 helps protect against drug toxicity and environmental chemicals.

> **Dietary Sources:** Wheatgrass juice, Barleygrass juice, Kamutgrass juice, Ryegrass juice, Oatgrass juice, Whole grains, Almonds, Brewer's yeast, Molasses, Broccoli, Green leafy vegetables, Yogurt, Soybeans, and Egg yolks.

> **Inhibits Absorption:** Alcohol, Tobacco, Coffee, and excessive Sugar. Pregnancy, Lactation, Excess dairy and Red meat consumption, Prolonged stress, Sulfa drugs, Diuretics, and Oral contraceptives all require extra Riboflavin.

> **Enhances Absorption:** Phosphorus, Niacin, Vitamins B-6, C, and B complex.

> **Deficiency Symptoms:** Associated with inflammation of the mouth, eye problems, dizziness, poor digestion, sore tongue, dermatitis, alcohol abuse, diabetes, ulcers, and congenital heart disease.

Niacin – Vitamin B-3

Niacin promotes normal growth in children and the proper functioning of the nervous system. Niacin is necessary in the maintenance of healthy skin, tongue, and a good digestive system. Niacin is also essential in metabolizing carbohydrates, fats, and protein. Vitamin B-3 can improve joints, and helps in lowering cholesterol. Niacin also works with chromium to help regulate blood sugar for diabetes and hypoglycemia.

Dietary Sources: Wheatgrass juice, Barleygrass juice, Kamutgrass juice, Ryegrass juice, Oatgrass juice, Beans, Whole wheat, Rice bran, Almonds, Brewer's yeast, Sesame seeds, Bananas, Avocados, Eggs, and Green vegetables.

Inhibits Absorption: Alcohol, Coffee, Excessive Sugar and Corn.

Enhances Absorption: Vitamins B-1, C, B Complex, and Phosphorus.

Deficiency Symptoms: Gastrointestinal disturbances, Dermatitis, Nervous disorders, Muscular aches, Loss of appetite, Insomnia, Tiredness, Halitosis, and Gum disease.

Pantothenic acid – Vitamin B-5

Pantothenic acid is an antioxidant vitamin and functions in the formation and building of antibodies. It is vital to proper adrenal activity. It works to prevent arthritis and high cholesterol. Vitamin B-5 helps build resistance toward stress, fatigue, and nerve disorders. Vitamin B-5 is vital for healthy adrenal glands, aids in energy, and stimulates normal growth in children.

Dietary Sources: Wheatgrass juice, Barleygrass juice, Kamutgrass juice, Ryegrass juice, Oatgrass juice, Whole grains, Wheat germ, Legumes, Brewer's yeast, Brown rice, Soy products, Yams, Egg yolks, Salmon, Orange juice, and Royal jelly.

Inhibits Absorption: Alcohol and Coffee.

Enhances Absorption: Sulfur, Vitamins C, B-6, B-12, B Complex, Folic acid, and Biotin.

Deficiency Symptoms: Stomach-stress, insulin sensitivity, eczema, hair loss, hypoglycemia, vomiting, diarrhea, kidney problems, anemia, and fatigue.

Pyridoxine – Vitamin B-6

Vitamin B-6 is necessary for carbohydrate, fat, and protein metabolism. It is key in red blood cell regeneration, it's an immune stimulant, and helps with antibody formation. Vitamin B-6 helps maintain all aspects of nerve health. It is also necessary for weight control and good for healthy skin and muscles. Vitamin B-6 is a must during pregnancy it can also help control nausea and vomiting during pregnancy. It is also necessary for the assimilation of magnesium. Vitamin B-6 may cause several problems if you are deficient.

Vitamin B-6 has also been used in the treatment of high cholesterol levels and in some heart disturbances.

Vitamin B-6 is water-soluble and is excreted from the body within eight hours of ingestion. Higher amounts are needed during pregnancy and lactation, or if one is on birth control pills. Those people who smoke, drink alcohol, or eat high protein diets also need a higher amount of vitamin B-6.

Dietary Sources: Wheatgrass juice, Barleygrass juice, Kamutgrass juice, Ryegrass juice, Oatgrass juice, Whole grains, Wheat germ, Buckwheat, Legumes, Nuts, Rice bran, Brown rice, Nuts, Brewer's yeast, Sunflower seeds, Soy foods, Molasses, Bananas, Avocados, Cantaloupe, Prunes, Cabbage, Peas, and Leafy green vegetables.

Inhibits Absorption: Alcohol, Tobacco, Coffee, Birth control pills, Thiazide diuretics, Penicillin,

Anti-rheumatic drug (Penicillamine), Hormone drugs (estrogen), and Radiation exposure.

Enhances Absorption: Linoleic acid, Sodium, Vitamins B-1, B-2, C, B Complex, Pantothenic acid, and Magnesium.

Deficiency Symptoms: Possible loss of muscle control, nervousness, dermatitis, insulin sensitivity, hair loss, mouth disorders, irritability, muscular weakness, convulsions in infants, depression, learning disabilities, anemia, arthritis, acne, and water retention.

Folic Acid – Folacin – Folate Vitamin B-9

Folic Acid is a B vitamin and is used in the synthesis of DNA, RNA, and enzyme production. It is necessary for the growth and production of red blood cells and has a fundamental role in the growth and reproduction of all cells. It is also necessary for healthy glands and liver. Folic Acid is critical following chemotherapy. It is a must during pregnancy to help prevent possible fetus damage and birth defects. It helps in the prevention of some complications during pregnancy such as: cleft palate, slow development, brain damage, premature delivery, afterbirth hemorrhaging and early placenta separation.

Folic acid is available from fresh unprocessed foods, which is why it is so commonly deficient in the US.

Dietary Sources: Wheatgrass juice, Barleygrass juice, Kamutgrass juice, Ryegrass juice, Oatgrass juice, Whole grains, Brown rice, Brewer's yeast, Soy foods, Corn, Lima beans, Green peas, Sweet potatoes, Artichokes, Okra, Parsnips Broccoli, Green leafy vegetables, Spinach, Kale, Beet greens and Beets, Fruits, Salmon, Eggs, and Bean sprouts such as Lentil, Mung, and Soybeans.

Inhibits Absorption: Alcohol, Tobacco, Coffee, Stress, Aluminum antacids, Oral contraceptives, Cholesterol-reducing drugs (Cholestyramine and Colestipol), Diuretic drugs (Potassium Sparing), GI anti-inflammatory drugs (p-Aminosalicylic Acid and Sulfasalazine), also many Anticonvulsants (Carbamazepine and Phenytonin), long term antibiotics, and anti-inflammatory drugs greatly increase the need for Folic Acid.

Enhances Absorption: Pantothenic acid, Vitamins C, B-12, B Complex, and Biotin.

Deficiency Symptoms: Gastrointestinal disorders, B-12 deficiency, anemia, and retarded growth in children.

Cyano Cobalamin
Vitamin B-12

Vitamin B-12 is called the "energy" vitamin, and is a necessary component for normal formation of red blood cells and is critical to DNA synthesis. Vitamin B-12 is involved in all immune responses. It is essential for the metabolism of the nerve tissue and promotes a healthy nervous system, good appetite, and healthy cells. Vitamin B-12 also helps with carbohydrate, fat, and protein metabolism. There is a greater need of vitamin B-12 during pregnancy.

Dietary Sources: Raw wheat germ, Sunflower seeds, Bee pollen, Alfalfa, Sea greens, Yogurt, Brewers yeast, Eggs, Cheese, Poultry, Fish, and Beef.

Inhibits Absorption: Alcohol, Tobacco, Coffee, and Laxatives. Long use of cholesterol drugs, oral contraceptives, anti-inflammatory and anti-convulsant drugs deplete B-12. Anti-rheumatic drug (Colchicine) GI anti-inflammatory drug (p-Amino-salicylic Acid). Deficiency can take five or more years to appear after the body stores are depleted.

Enhance Absorption: B Complex, Folic acid, Vitamins B-6, C, Choline, Inositol, Sodium, and Potassium.

Deficiency Symptoms: Tiredness, general weakness, poor appetite, speaking difficulties, anemia, nervousness, neuritis, brain damage, growth reduction in children, nerve degeneration, and heart palpitations.

Vitamin A – Beta Carotene (Plant sources) Vitamin A - Retinol (Animal sources)

Vitamin A is important for healthy formation of bones, teeth, and skin. It is also necessary for the maintenance of the outer layers of many tissues and organs. Vitamin A promotes normal growth and vitality and is good for night vision. It helps develop strong bone cells, a major factor in the health of hair, skin, teeth, and gums. Vitamin A is an antioxidant that helps protect the body from the effects of free radicals.

> **Dietary Sources:** Wheatgrass juice, Barleygrass juice, Kamutgrass juice, Ryegrass juice, Oatgrass juice, Black beans, Blackeye peas, Garbanzo beans, Soybeans, Mung beans, Split peas, Pumpkin and Squash seeds, Barley, Yellow fruits and vegetables, carrots Dark leafy greens, Fish liver oils, Fish, Sea greens, and eggs.

> **Inhibits Absorption:** Alcohol, Coffee, Cholesterol reducing drugs (Cholestyramine and Colestipol), Excessive iron, Mineral oil, and Vitamin D deficiency.

> **Enhance Absorption:** Vitamins C, D, E, F, B Complex, Calcium, Choline, and Zinc. Vitamin A is fat soluble, requiring fats, minerals (especially

zinc) and enzymes for absorption.

Deficiency Symptoms: Defective teeth and gums, allergies, dry hair, retarded growth in children, susceptibility to infections, eye irritations, inability to tear, and night blindness, sinus trouble, dry skin, and loss of smell.

Vitamin D – Calciferol

Vitamin D is called the "sun shine" vitamin. It is really a hormone produced in the skin from sunlight. It works with Vitamin A to utilize calcium and phosphorus in building bones and teeth. Vitamin D is very important in infancy and childhood in building healthy bone formation. Vitamin D is necessary in maintenance for a healthy thyroid gland, skin, teeth, nervous system maintenance and normal blood clotting. Vitamin D helps with eye problems including spots, conjunctivitis, and glaucoma. Twenty minutes a day of early morning sunshine makes a real difference to your body's vitamin D store-house, especially if you are at risk for osteoporosis.

Dietary Sources: Cod liver oil, Yogurt, Butter, Salmon, Tuna, Sardines, Egg yolks, and Bone meal.

Inhibits Absorption: Mineral oil, Cholesterol-reducing drugs (Cholestyramine and Colestipol) and Anticonvulsants (Carbamazepine and Phenytonin).

Enhances Absorption: Phosphorus, Selenium, Manganese, Inositol, Vitamins A, B-1, C, F, and B Complex.

Deficiency Symptoms: May lead to rickets, lack of vigor, muscle weakness, inadequate absorption of calcium, phosphorus retention in the kidneys, diarrhea, insomnia, nervousness, soft bones and teeth, nearsighted, muscle cramps and tics.

Vitamin E
Tocopherol / Tocopheryl

Vitamin E is an immune stimulating vitamin. It protects fat-soluble vitamins and red blood cells, prevents blood clots, and maintains healthy muscles and nerves. Vitamin E strengthens capillary walls and is necessary for good hair, skin, and mucous membranes. Vitamin A and E together can help to decrease cholesterol and general fat accumulation. Vitamin E retards cellular and mental aging. And helps in healing of wounds and burns. Vitamin E helps to fight tumors. It also helps to neutralize free radicals and to prevent them from damaging cell membranes in the eyes.

Frying oils, processing and milling of foods, the bleaching of flours, and cooking removes much of the vitamin E content of whole foods.

Dietary Sources: Wheatgrass juice, Barleygrass juice, Kamutgrass juice, Ryegrass juice, Oatgrass juice, Whole wheat, Wheat germ, Wheat germ oil, Almonds, Hazelnuts, Pecans, Sunflower seeds, Sunflower seed oil, Soybeans, Flaxseed, Nuts, Molasses, Sweet potatoes, Dark green leafy vegetables, Brown rice, Barley, Rye, Oats, Buckwheat, and Amaranth.

Inhibits Absorption: Mineral oil, Rancid fat & oil, Chlorine, Birth control pills, and Cholesterol-reducing drugs (Cholestyramine and Colestipol).

Enhances Absorption: Phosphorous, Selenium, Manganese, Inositol, Vitamins A, B-1, C, F, and B Complex.

Deficiency Symptoms: Fragility of red blood cells, dry dull hair, sterility, impotency, miscarriages, gastrointestinal problems, heart disease, enlarged prostrate, muscle and nerve degeneration.

Amino Acids

Amino Acids

Amino acids are the building blocks of protein in the body. Amino acids are necessary to life, growth, and healing. There are 29 known amino acids at this time, which form over 1600 basic proteins. The liver produces about 80% of the amino acids it needs; the remaining 20% must come from food. Listed are the main amino acids. The body cannot produce essential amino acids, this is why they are called essential and must be provided to the body.

The eight essential amino acids:
These are the amino acids that our body must get from food in order to produce the "non-essential" amino acids. Our bodies cannot make these amino acids.

Tryptophan	Threonine	Isoleucine
Leucine	Lysine	Methionine
Phenylalanine	Valine	

The semi-essential amino acids:
These amino acids can only be produced by the body if we consume the eight essential amino acids.

Arginine	Cysteine	Cystine
Histidine	Tyrosine	

The non-essential amino acids:

Alanine	Asparagine	Aspartic acid
Carnitine	Citrulline	Glutamic acid
Glutamine	Glycine	Ornithine
Taurine	Proline	Serine

Amino Acids Used in Clinical Practice

Tryptophan is used for sleep and anxiety disorders. As of today it is the only known substance that can be converted into the neurotransmitter called serotonin. It helps in the formation of neurotransmitters that transmit nerve impulses within the brain and the nervous system.

Lysine is used in Herpes simplex treatment & prevention. Lysine has broad immune-enhancing effects. It helps maintain nitrogen balance and calcium absorption in adults. It's instrumental in collagen formation, which helps insure healthy connective tissue, skin, cartilage and bone.

Amino Acid	Used For:
DL-phenylalanine	Pain
L-carnitine	Weight loss, cardiovascular disease
L-arginine/L-ornithine	Bodybuilding
L-cysteine	Antioxidant, detoxifier
L-taurine	Depression, convulsions
L-glutamine	Alcohol and sugar cravings/ addictions
L-tyrosine	Depression

Methionine is considered to be one of the body's most powerful detoxifying agents. It helps to protect the cells from environmental pollutants, in the transportation and absorption of selenium and zinc in the body and helps prevent the buildup of excess fat in the liver.

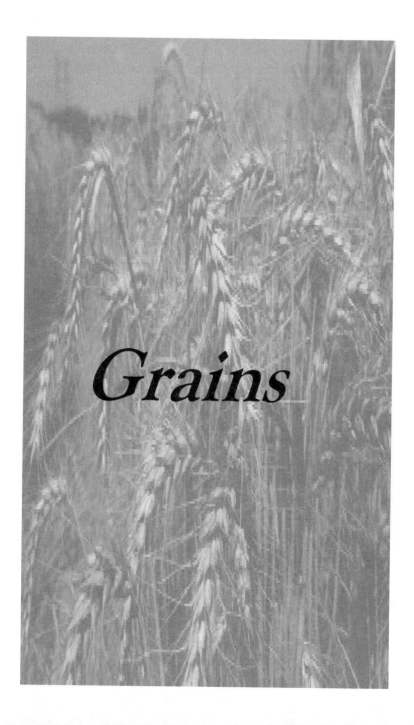

Grains

Hard Red Winter Wheat   **Soft Red Winter Wheat**

Hard Red Spring Wheat   **Durum Wheat**

Soft White Winter Wheat   **Hard White Winter**

Soft White Spring Wheat   **Club Wheat**

Spelt   **Kamut**

White Oats | Red Oats

Oat Groats | Rye

Hulled Barley | Pearled Barley

Amaranth | Quinoa

Millet Hulled | Corn

Whole Buckwheat   **Hulled Buckwheat**

Green Lentiles   **Red Lentiles**

Brown Flaxseed   **Golden Flaxseed**

Short Brown Rice   **Long Brown Rice**

Long White Rice   **Soybeans**

Adzuki Beans

Mung Beans

Fenugreek Seeds

Alfalfa Seeds

Whole Sunflower Seeds

Shelled Sunflower Seeds

Black Beans

Black-eyed Peas

Garbanzo Beans

Kidney Beans

Grains
The Choices are Yours

Whole wheat and whole grains promote regularity and give us the vital nutrients that have been removed from processed foods. During the modern processing of wheat 50 to 87 percent of the nutrients are lost.

Wheat can be a mucus forming grain, and for some people without optimal health, they seem not to be able to assimilate whole wheat as well or they seem to develop an allergic reaction to wheat. There may be other underling reasons for this such as the chemicals used in crop production, the yeast, which is added to most bread that contributes to this situation, insufficient quantity of digestive enzymes in some individuals, or other reasons. Variety will be the key. Learn to add different grains to your wheat. You should use a five to one ratio most of the time when baking breads. Use five parts Wheat, Spelt, or Kamut to one part other grains.

For those who have sensitivity to wheat they can usually tolerate Spelt or Kamut. Spelt is an ancient red wheat that many people can tolerate that have wheat allergies. Spelt can be ground into flour and used for making breads and other baked goods. Kamut is a strain of wheat that has not been cross-bred and hybridized as much as traditional wheat. Kamut like Spelt has been used by people with wheat allergies with great success. Kamut can be ground into flour and used instead of whole wheat.

Triticale is a genetic cross between wheat and rye. When

using this grain instead of wheat you should not use equal substitution. Triticale should not exceed half the wheat flour called for in a recipe, because the gluten does not form as in whole wheat.

Grains that are Alkalizing are Amaranth, Buckwheat, Hulled Millet, and Quinoa. There are many books written on the subject of acid vs. alkaline in our system and the balancing of them. The main message in all writings is that disease can not grow in an alkaline pH balanced system and that Acid conditions have been linked to diseases as common as the flu and as chronic as arthritis, fungal growths and cancer.

When wheat is soaked and used as Bulgar wheat or when sprouting, there is an increase of enzymes released that are necessary for digestion.

Wheat is still the most essential grain to store. It is to be used for sprouting and grown to become wheat grass, which is to be used for juicing. In these forms it becomes beneficial to all. Wheat grass juice has a similar molecular structure as hemin in our hemoglobin that carries the vital oxygen throughout our body. The hard red winter Wheat and Kamut, along with Oats, Barley, and Rye should be stored for sprouting and grown into grasses for juicing as well as used as cereals and baking. Soft wheat is good for pastries and a drink called rejuvelac, which is used in most natural cancer clinics. Brown Rice, Barley, Rye, and Oats help remove cholesterol from the body, and Amaranth is a nutritional giant for such a small grain and one of the few grains that contain measurable vitamin C with out sprouting.

In the deciding process of how much and which grains to store, two things to consider; one Wheat is the staff of life and has been known to store well over fifty years. You as an adult would need 400 pounds of wheat and 60 pounds of Legumes which includes beans: soy, pinto, lima, kidney, white, red, navy, pink, black-eyed, etc. also lentils, and nuts, to sustain life for one year.

The other thing to consider is sensitivity to regular wheat, variety, textures, and that other grains are needed for balanced nutrition, if you are not sprouting and juicing your wheat.

An excellent combination are the grains found in Ezekiel Bread (Ezekiel 4:9). They are Wheat, Barley, Beans, Lentils, Millet and Fitches (Spelt which is an ancient wheat and available today). Two recipes I have used for Ezekiel Bread one substitutes Rye for Spelt the other substitutes White Wheat or it is also called Pastry Wheat or Spring Wheat for Spelt. One of the recipes just calls for beans the other uses Pinto Beans and Soybeans. I have also used Spelt as stated in Ezekiel 4:9.

You need to plan on adding a variety of grains to your storage. Grains are made to be mixed. For babies an excellent combination is Brown Rice, Millet, Barley and Oat Groates. These grains are very mild and easy to digest. They are also excellent for older adults who have a problem with digestion. You would combine equal parts of each grain.

Another combination of grains that can be used for breads, pancakes, waffles, or ground to add to your favorite recipes calling for flour are Wheat, Amaranth, Hulled Barley, Hulled Buckwheat, Corn, Millet, Brown Rice, Rye, and Oat Groates. You would use a five to one ratio. That means; for every cup of other grains you would add five cups of wheat. The wheat could be any combination of hard, soft, or ancient wheats.

When combining grains for cooked cereal I combine one cup of every grain I have. Then I would grind them to a course cracked state. I use one quarter cup ground grain to one cup distilled cold water and cook like regular hot cereal. I can then use this same combination in baking breads by grinding these grains into flour and adding the additional wheat that is needed. Again using the five to one ratio adding the additional wheat for baking.

Be wise in choosing your grains. You could choose to store 350 pounds of wheat per person and 75 pounds of other grains. You will eventually use all your wheat through sprouting and juicing. You may also cut your wheat to 300 pounds per person and add 150 pounds of the other grains. The majority of your grain should be some kind of wheat, although you should combine your grains into one grain for the maximum benefit.

It has been stated that "all grain is" good for the food of man. It was not stated "all grains are" good. The interpretation is to combine your grains, that they should be made into one grain for the good of man. In doing this you will promote better health.

Whole Wheat

Wheat King of the grains and ranks first in nutritional value is our most important grain. Whole Wheat is rich in **protein, minerals, amino acids and vitamins.** When Wheat is sprouted, you get the added nutrient of vitamin C and live enzymes. When wheat grass is juiced you really find that wheat is really the staff of life. Wheat also contains Calcium. Calcium can not be assimilated in the body properly with out Magnesium which wheat contains. This is so essential to our bones. There are so many nutrients in Wheat that is essential to our good health. Whole wheat bread contains approximately 4 times more fiber than white bread.

Vitamin E in Whole Wheat is a powerful element for the heart, muscles, and the reproductive system. Vitamin E helps build strong muscles and tones the kidneys. It is also essential in helping the brain, the nervous system, and emotional stability. Chinese say it nourishes the heart and mind.

There are several varieties that store well some are hard red winter wheat, spring wheat, red wheat, Kamut, Spelt, and Montana white wheat. What ever type you store the moisture content should be 10% or less. I have been able to get 3% at times. The protein content will also very, you should store no less than 16%, but preferably much higher.

Properly stored wheat will store almost indefinitely. The

way to check your wheat is to take a couple of tablespoons full, and if it will sprout you still have good wheat. Wheat that is dead will not make a good light loaf of bread. Poorly stored wheat will loose it's food value, and will have little benefit.

One cup of Hard Red Winter Wheat contains the following:

Protein 24.2g   **Carbohydrate** 136.6g
Fiber 23.4g   **Ash** 3.0g

Minerals:
Calcium 55.6mg   Iron 6.1mg
Phosphorus 552.9mg   Zinc 5.0mg
Potassium 696.9 mg   Sodium 3.8mg
Magnesium 241.9mg   Copper 0.8mg
Manganese 7.6mg

Vitamins:
Thiamin 0.7mg   Riboflavin 0.2mg
Niacin 10.4mg   Vit. B-6 0.5mg
Folate 72.9mcg   Vit. E 2.7mg_ATE
Pantothenic acid 1.8mg

Amino acids:
Tryptophan 0.3g   Threonine 0.7g   Isoleucine 0.8g
Leucine 1.6g   Lysine 0.6g   Methionine 0.3g
Cystine 0.6g   Valine 1.0g   Tyrosine 0.7g
Phenylalanine 1.1g   Arginine 1.1g   Histidine 0.5g
Alanine .8g   Serine 1.1g   Proline 2.4g
Aspartic acid 1.2g   Glycine 1.0g
Glutamine acid 7.6g

Millet

 Millet Queen of the grains, contains all essential amino acids, high in minerals and vitamins, and is high in protein. Millet is **alkaline** and easy to digest. It can also help to build superior health and physique. Millet helps the kidneys, stomach, spleen, and pancreas. Millet is the best grain for relieving Candida in our systems. Millet is very low in gluten and does not feed the yeast. Millet can be used in breads, soups, puddings, and casseroles. Use the one to five ratio of millet to wheat in making bread. Too much millet in bread makes a very dense bread and the top crust peels off.

The Hunzas in the Himalayan Mountains, which are known for there great health and long life span use a great deal of millet in their diets.

One cup of Millet contains the following:

Protein 22g   **Carbohydrate** 146g   **Fiber** 17g   **Ash** 6g

Minerals:

Calcium 16mg	Selenium 5mcg	Iron 6mg
Phosphorus 570mg	Potassium 390 mg	Zinc 3mg
Sodium 10mg	Magnesium 228mg	Copper 2mg
Manganese 3mg		

Vitamins:

Thiamin 0.8mg	Riboflavin 0.6mg	Niacin 9mg

Vit. B-6 0.8mg   Folate 170mcg
Vit. E 0.4mg_ATE   Tocopherol .1mg
Pantothenic acid 2mg

Amino acids:

Tryptophan 0.2g	Threonine 0.7g	Isoleucine 0.9g
Leucine 3g	Lysine 0.4g	Methionine 0.4g
Cystine 0.4g	Phenylalanine 1g	Tyrosine 0.7g
Valine 1g	Arginine 0.8g	Histidine 0.5g
Alanine 2g	Glutamine acid 5g	Serine 1g
Glycine 0.6g	Aspartic acid 1g	Proline 2g

Brown Rice

Brown Rice contains many B Vitamins, thiamin, niacin, riboflavin, potassium and carbohydrates, phosphorous, magnesium, calcium, and all eight of the essential amino acids. Great body builder. Good for bones, teeth, nervous system, mental depression, nausea, diarrhea, and diabetes. Brown rice does not store as long as white rice because of its oil content, but if stored properly will last a long time. When rice is sproutted it contains Vitamin C.

Brown rice can be used as breakfast cereals, cream of rice, casseroles, and can be made into flour to be used in breads, and cookies. Of course it can be steamed or boiled to go along with or be the main stay of a meal. Amazake made from Sweet Brown Rice is a tasty milk substitute, which is both rich and sweet.

There are several varieties of brown rice. Short Grain Brown Rice is preferred for casseroles and hardy dishes. Long Grain Brown Rice is used more for pilafs, entrees, and salads. Brown Basmati is a long grain rice with a nutty aroma. It seems to be easier to digest than other varieties of brown rice. Sweet Brown Rice is higher in protein and fat than other rice and is recommended for nursing mothers.

Rice is not as high in protein as wheat and some other grains, but the protein is a good quality and easily utilized.

One cup of Brown Rice contains the following:

Protein 15g   **Carbohydrate** 143g   **Fiber** 6g   **Ash** 3g

Minerals:

Calcium 43mg	Magnesium 265mg
Phosphorus 616mg	Iron 3mg
Potassium 413 mg	Sodium 13mg
Zinc 4mg	Copper 0.5mg
Manganese 7mg	Selenium 43mcg

Vitamins:

Thiamin 0.7mg	Riboflavin 0.2mg	Niacin 9mg
Pantothenic acid 3mg	Vit. B-6 0.9mg	Folate 37mcg
Vit. E 1mg_ATE	Tocopherol 1mg	

Amino acids:

Tryptophan 0.2g	Threonine 05g	Isoleucine 0.6g
Leucine 1g	Lysine 0.6g	Methionine 0.3g
Cystine 0.2g	Phenylalanine 1g	Tyrosine 0.6g
Valine 0.9g	Arginine 1g	Histidine 0.4g
Alanine 1g	Aspartic acid 1g	Glutamine acid 3g
Glycine 0.7g	Proline 0.7g	Serine 0.8g

White Rice

White rice if stored properly will last eight to ten years. This is because the rice has been refined, or polished. The rice is then bleached, cleaned, pearled, and often oiled and coated. This may make the rice more pleasing to the eye, however now the rice has lost the oils and a great deal of the nutrients has been decreased.

One cup of Long-grain white Rice contains the following:

Protein 13g   **Carbohydrate** 148g   **Fiber** 2g   **Ash** 1g

Minerals:

Calcium 32mg	Magnesium 46mg
Phosphorus 213mg	Iron 1mg
Potassium 213 mg	Sodium 9mg
Zinc 2mg	Copper 0.4mg
Manganese 2mg	Selenium 28mcg

Vitamins:

Thiamin 0.1mg	Riboflavin 0.09mg	Niacin 3mg
Pantothenic acid 2mg	Vit. B-6 0.3mg	Folate 15mcg
Vit. E 0.2mg_ATE	Tocopherol 0mg	

Amino acids:

Tryptophan 0.2g	Threonine 0.5g	Leucine1g
Isoleucine 0.6g	Lysine 0.5g	Methionine 0.3g
Cystine 0.3g	Phenylalanine 1g	Tyrosine 0.4g
Valine 0.8g	Arginine 1g	Histidine 0.3g
Alanine 1g	Aspartic acid 1g	Proline 0.6g
Glutamine acid 3g	Glycine 0.6g	Serine 0.7g

Barley

 Barley contains Calcium, Iron, Protein, Vitamin A, and is a source of tocotrienols (an antioxidant). It is good for nerves, muscles, spleen, and pancreas. The nutrients in Barley also help to keep joints limber. Barley is great in soups and pilafs. It can be ground into flour and used in breads in place of wheat.

One cup of Barley contains the following:

Protein 23g   **Carbohydrate** 135g   **Fiber** 32g   **Ash** 4g

Minerals:
Calcium 61mg   Iron 7mg   Magnesium 245mg
Phosphorus 486mg   Zinc 5mg   Sodium 22mg
Potassium 832mg   Copper 0.9mg   Manganese 4mg
Selenium 28mcg

Vitamins:
Thiamin 1mg   Riboflavin 0.5mg   Niacin 8mg
Vit. B-6 0.6mg   Vit. A, 40IU   Vit A 4mcg_RE
Folate 35mcg   Vit. E 1mg_ATE   Tocopherol 1mg
Pantothenic acid 0.5mg

Amino acids:
Tryptophan 0.4g   Threonine 0.8g   Isoleucine 0.8g
Leucine 2g   Lysine 0.9g   Methionine 0.4g
Cystine 0.5g   Phenylalanine 1g   Tyrosine 0.7g
Valine 1g   Arginine 1g   Histidine 0.5g
Alanine 1g   Aspartic acid 1g   Glycine 0.8g
Glutamine acid 6g   Proline 3g   Serine 1g

Corn

Corn contains Magnesium, Iron, Proteins, Carbohydrates, Potassium, and Magnesium, which help the  bowel and is necessary for good tone in the intestinal tract. Corn is also good for the heart, stomach, teeth, and gums. Corn however should be used in moderation.

One cup of Whole grain **White Corn** does not contain the Vitamin A listed and the fiber is 11g.

One cup of Whole grain **Yellow Corn** contains the following:

Protein 8g   **Carbohydrate** 90g   **Fiber** 16g   **Ash** 2g

Minerals:

Calcium 8mg	Iron 3mg	Magnesium 109mg
Phosphorus 318mg	Sodium 6mg	Potassium 368 mg
Manganese 5mg	Zinc 2mg	Copper 0.3mg
Selenium 18mcg		

Vitamins:

Thiamin 0.3mg	Riboflavin 0.09mg	Niacin 2mg
Vit. B-6 0.4mg	Folate 29mcg	Vit. A, 549 IU
Vit. E 1mg_ATE	Tocopherol 1mg	Vit A 55mcg_RE
Pantothenic acid 0.08mg		

Amino acids:

Tryptophan 0.05g   Threonine 0.3g   Isoleucine 0.3g
Leucine 1g   Lysine 0.2g   Cystine 0.1g
Methionine 0.2g   Valine 0.4g   Glycine 0.3g
Phenylalanine 0.4g   Serine 0.4g   Tyrosine 0.3g
Arginine 0.4g   Histidine 0.2g   Alanine 1g
Aspartic acid 1g   Glutamine acid 2g
Proline 0.7g

Rye

Rye is a great muscle builder; it contains Vitamin E,
 Phosphorous, and Magnesium. Rye is also
good for the heart, muscles, and the liver,
the reproductive system, gallbladder, and
the spleen, pancreas, digestive system, and
prevention of vessel and plaque calcifica-
tion. When Rye is sprouted it contains a
natural fluoride. The broth has been used for
migraine headaches.

Pure rye bread is a very nutritious moist dense black bread.
It is also excellent as a supplementary grain to wheat. Two
parts rye to five parts wheat makes an excellent light rye
bread. Rye is good added to recipes calling for corn or
oatmeal as part of the flour.

Cooked Rye berries may be added to salads, casseroles,
and pilafs.

One cup of Whole grain Rye contains the following:

Protein 25g   **Carbohydrate** 118g   **Fiber** 25g   **Ash** 3g

Minerals:
Calcium 56mg   Iron 5mg   Zinc 6mg
Phosphorus 632mg   Potassium 446 mg Sodium 10mg
Magnesium 204mg   Copper 0.8mg   Selenium 60mcg
Manganese 5mg

Vitamins:

Thiamin 0.5mg   Riboflavin 0.4mg   Niacin 7mg
Pantothenic acid 2mg   Vit. B-6 0.5mg   Folate 101mcg
Vit. E 3mg_ATE   Tocopherol 2mg   Vit. A, 0 IU
Vit A 0mcg_RE

Amino acids:

Tryptophan 0.3g   Threonine 0.9g   Isoleucine 0.9g
Leucine 2g   Lysine 1g   Methionine 0.4g
Cystine 0.6g   Phenylalanine 1g   Tyrosine 0.6g
Valine 1g   Arginine 1g   Histidine 0.6g
Alanine 1g   Aspartic acid 2g   Glutamine acid 6g
Glycine 1g   Proline 3g   Serine 1g

Oats

Oats contain Thiamin, Niacin, Riboflavin, Protein, Fat, Iodine, and Calcium. Oats are good for muscles, brain, spleen, nerve structure, pancreas, reproductive system, bones and connective tissue. Oats help remove cholesterol from our system, helps ease constipation by adding bulk to our system, and it has been known to help stabilize blood-sugar levels. It has also been used as a poultice to relieve itching and as a tea to help strengthen the immune system.

One cup of Whole grain Oats contains the following:

Protein 26g   **Carbohydrate** 103g   **Fiber** 17g   **Ash** 3g

Minerals:

Calcium 84mg   Iron 7mg   Magnesium 276mg
Phosphorus 815mg   Zinc 6mg   Sodium 3mg
Potassium 669 mg   Copper 1mg   Manganese 8mg
Selenium 0mcg

Vitamins:

Thiamin 1mg   Riboflavin 0.2mg   Niacin 1mg
Pantothenic acid 2mg   Vit. B-6 0.2mg   Folate 87mcg
Vit. E 1mg_ATE   Tocopherol 0mg
Vit. A, 0 IU   Vit A 0mcg_RE

Amino acids:

Tryptophan 0.4g	Threonine 0.9g	Isoleucine 1g
Leucine 2g	Lysine 1g	Methionine 0.5g
Cystine 0.6g	Phenylalanine 1g	Tyrosine 0.9g
Valine 1g	Arginine 2g	Histidine 0.6g
Alanine 1g	Aspartic acid 2g	Glutamine acid 6g
Glycine 1g	Proline 1g	Serine 1g

Buckwheat

Buckwheat is rich in minerals and Vitamins, Vitamin E, B complex, Starch, Fat, Protein and Rutin. Buckwheat strengthens the arterial walls, reduces blood pressure and assists in relieving varicose veins. Buckwheat cleans and strengthens the intestines, and is used in combating dysentery and diarrhea. Rutin has been used as an antidote against some radiation. Buckwheat is also low in gluten and does not feed the yeast in our systems.

One cup of Buckwheat contains the following:

Protein 23g   **Carbohydrate** 122g   **Fiber** 17g   **Ash** 4g

Minerals:
Calcium 31mg   Iron 4mg   Manganese 2mg
Phosphorus 590mg   Zinc 4mg   Sodium 2mg
Potassium 782mg   Copper 2mg   Selenium 14mcg
Magnesium 393mg

Vitamins:
Thiamin 0.2mg   Riboflavin 0.7mg   Niacin 12mg
Vit. A, 0 IU   Vit. B-6 0.4mg   Folate 51mcg
Vit. E 2mg_ATE   Tocopherol 0mg
Vit A 0mcg_RE   Pantothenic acid 2mg

Amino acids:
Tryptophan 0.3g   Threonine 0.9g   Isoleucine 0.8g
Leucine 1g   Lysine 1g   Methionine 0.3g

Serine 1g   Cystine 0.4g   Tyrosine 0.4g
Valine 1g   Arginine 2g   Histidine 0.5g
Alanine 1g   Aspartic acid 2g   Glutamine acid 3g
Glycine 2g   Proline 1g   Phenylalanine 1g

Amaranth

Amaranth is high in Protein, Calcium and Vitamin C. It contains more calcium than milk and is utilized very efficiently because of its Magnesium content. It has been helpful for nursing or pregnant women, infants, and children, or those who do heavy physical work. Amaranth is an **alkaline**-forming grain and is very low in gluten, so it does not feed the yeast in our systems.

Amaranth is used whole when cooked as cereal or side dishes. It is also ground into flour for breads, cookies, pastas, or tortillas.

One cup of Whole grain Amaranth contains the following:

Protein 28g   **Carbohydrate** 129g   **Fiber** 30g   **Ash** 6g

Minerals:

Calcium 298mg	Iron 15mg	Selenium 0mcg
Phosphorus 887mg	Sodium 41mg	Copper 2mg
Potassium 714mg	Zinc 6mg	Manganese 4mg
Magnesium 519mg		

Vitamins:

Thiamin 0.2mg	Riboflavin 0.4mg	Niacin 3mg
Vit. C 8mg	Vit. B-6 0.4mg	Folate 96mcg
Vit. E 2mg_ATE	Pantothenic acid 2mg	

Amino acids:

Tryptophan 0.4g   Threonine 1g   Isoleucine 1g
Leucine 2g   Lysine 1g   Methionine 0.4g
Cystine 0.4g   Tyrosine 0.6g   Glycine 3g
Valine 1g   Arginine 2g   Histidine 0.8g
Alanine 2g   Serine 2g   Glutamine acid 4g
Aspartic acid 2g   Proline 1g   Phenylalanine 1g

Quinoa
(Pronounced "keen-wah")

Quinoa, also known as Inca wheat and is a cousin to Amaranth. It contains most of the same nutritional quailties except for Vitamin C. Quinoa is also low in gluten and does not feed the yeast in our systems. Quinoa is an alkaline-forming grain and therefore contributes to our over all health. It is very beneficial for our bodies to be slightly alkaline. Quinoa is used in making breads and is eaten in salads.

One cup of Whole grain Quinoa contains the following:

Protein 22g   **Carbohydrate** 117g   **Fiber** 10g   **Ash** 5g

Minerals:

Calcium 102mg	Iron 16mg	Magnesium 357mg
Phosphorus 697mg	Zinc 6mg	Sodium 36mg
Potassium 1258mg	Copper 1mg	Manganese 4mg

Vitamins:

Thiamin 0.3mg	Riboflavin 0.7mg	Niacin 5mg
Pantothenic acid 2mg	Vit. B-6 0.4mg	Folate 83mcg

Amino acids:

Tryptophan 0g	Threonine 1g	Leucine 1g
Lysine 1g	Proline 1g	Cystine 0g
Phenylalanine 1g	Serine 1g	Valine 1g
Histidine 0.5g	Alanine 1g	Arginine 2g
Isoleucine 1g	Aspartic acid 2g	Glycine 1g
Glutamine acid 3g	Methionine 0.4g	Tyrosine 0.6g

Spelt & Kamut

Spelt is an ancient wheat and Kamut is a strain of wheat. Both of these wheats can be used by the majority of gluten-sensitive individuals without adverse side affects. Both grains can be used alone to make breads and cereals or they can be added to regular wheat or other grains.

Triticale

Triticale is a grain that has been genetically crossed between wheat and rye. Triticale needs to be added to wheat in a one to one ratio in order to make a good loaf of bread.

Beans and Other Legumes
The Choices are Yours

Beans are packed with Minerals, Vitamins, Amino acids, and Protein. They are a rich source of protein. Together with rice they make a complete protein containing all eight essential amino acids.

An easy way to bottle beans and have them ready for quick and easy recipes, is to put one cup of dry beans in each one-quart canning jar. Fill each jar with distilled water and let them sit overnight. In the morning, drain the water from the jars. Rinse the beans with clean water, and drain well, do not remove the beans from the jars. Cover the jars with a towel. Repeat this process in the evening washing and draining the beans well, again cover the jars with a towel. The following morning, again rinse and drain the beans. Then fill each jar with water (I prefer distilled water) to the neck and add 1tsp salt. Boil the canning lids and wiping the top of the jar place the lid on the jar adjust and tighten lids. You will then pressure cook the beans at 13lbs. presser for 1 ½ hours. **NOTE:** The one-cup of beans in each bottle will never leave that bottle during the entire process. They will swell and sprout to fill the jar.

Another way to add beans to your diet is to grind them into flour. You can add a few tablespoons of bean flour to commercial cake mixes, pancake mixes, or more preferably to your own home made nutritional mixes.

Sprouting beans gives more variety and nutrition to your diet.

Adzuki Beans

Excellent for sprouting. When used in cooking combine with either rice or millet in a 1 to 3 ratio (beans to grain) it will provide a lower amount of gas while providing a complete protein.

One cup of Adzuki contains the following:

Protein 39.1g   **Carbohydrate** 123.9g
Fiber 25.0g   **Ash** 6.4g

Minerals:
Calcium 130.0mg   Iron 9.8mg   Sodium 9.8mg
Phosphorus 750.5mg   Zinc 9.9mg   Copper 2.1mg
Manganese 3.4mg   Selenium 6.1mcg
Magnesium 250.1mg   Potassium K 2470.3 mg

Vitamins:
Thiamin 0.8mg   Riboflavin 0.4mg   Niacin 5.1mg
Vit.B-6 0.6mg   Folate 1225.3mcg   Vit A 33.4 IU
Pantothenic acid 2.8mg

Amino acids:
Tryptophan 0.3g   Threonine 1.3g   Serine 1.9g
Leucine 3.2g   Lysine 2.9g   Cystine 0.3g
Phenylalanine 2.0g   Valine 2.0g   Glycine 1.4g
Arginine 2.5g   Histidine 1.0g   Alanine 2.2g
Aspartic acid 4.6g   Isoleucine 1.5g   Proline 1.7g
Glutamic acid 6.1g   Methionine 0.4g   Tyrosine 1.1g

Black Beans

High in Calcium, Magnesium, Potassium, and Protein.

One cup of Black beans contains the following:

Protein 41.9g   **Carbohydrate** 120.9g
Fiber 29.4g   **Ash** 6.9g

Minerals:
Calcium 238.6mg   Iron 9.7mg
Phosphorus 682.8mg   Sodium 9.7mg
Magnesium 331.7mg   Zinc 7.0mg
Potassium 2877.0mg   Copper 1.6mg
Manganese 2.0mg   Selenium 6.2mcg

Vitamins:
Thiamin 1.78mg   Riboflavin 0.3mg
Pantothenic acid 1.7mg   Niacin 3.7mg
Vit. B-6 0.5mg   Folate 861.3mcg
Vit. A32.9 IU   Vit. E 0.4mg_ATE

Amino acids:
Tryptophan 0.4g   Threonine 1.7g   Isoleucine 1.8g
Leucine 3.3g   Lysine 2.8g   Cystine 0.4g
Methionine 0.6g   Tyrosine 1.1g   Valine 2.1g
Arginine 2.5g   Histidine 1.1g   Alanine 1.7g
Aspartic acid 5.0g   Glycine 1.6g   Serine 2.2g
Glutamic acid 6.3g   Proline 1.77g
Phenylalanine 2.2g

Blackeye peas, Cowpeas, Crowder, or called Southern peas

One cup of Cowpeas contains the following:

Protein 39.2g　　　　　**Carbohydrate** 100.2g
Fiber 17.7g　　　　　　**Ash** 5.4g

Minerals:

Calcium 183.7mg　　　　Iron 13.8mg
Magnesium 307.2mg　　　Phosphorus 708.0mg
Potassium 1857.0 mg　　　Sodium 26.7mg
Manganese 2.5mg　　　　Zinc 5.6mg
Selenium 15.0mcg　　　　Copper 1.4mg

Vitamins:

Thiamin 1.4mg　　　　　Riboflavin 0.3mg
Pantothenic acid 2.4mg　　Niacin 3.4mg
Vit. B-6 0.5mg　　　　　Folate 1057.1mcg
Vit. E 0.6mg_ATE　　　　Vit. C 2.5mg
Vit. A 83.5 IU

Amino acids:

Tryptophan 0.4g　　Threonine 1.4g　　Isoleucine 1.5g
Leucine 3.0g　　　　Lysine 2.6g　　　Methionine 0.5g
Cystine 0.4g　　　　Tyrosine 1.2g　　Valine 1.8g
Arginine 2.7g　　　Histidine 1.2g　　Alanine 1.7g
Aspartic acid 4.7g　Glycine 1.6g　　Serine 1.9g
Glutamic acid 7.4g　Proline 1.7g
Phenylalanine 2.2g

Chickpeas also called Garbanzo Beans and Bengal Gram

Chickpeas are very high in fiber.

One cup of Chickpeas contains the following:

Protein 38.6g   **Carbohydrate** 121.3g
Fiber 34.8g   **Ash** 4.9g

Minerals:
Calcium 210.0mg   Iron 12.4mg
Magnesium 230.0mg   Phosphorus 732.0mg
Potassium 1750.7mg   Sodium 48.0mg
Zinc 6.8mg   Copper 1.6mg
Manganese 4.4mg   Selenium 16.4mcg

Vitamins:
Thiamin 0.9mg   Riboflavin 0.4mg
Niacin 3.8mg   Pantothenic acid 3.1mg
Vit. B-6 1.0mg   Folate 1114.0mcg
Vit. E 1.6mg_ATE   Vit. A 134.0 IU
Vit. C 8.0mg

Amino acids:
Tryptophan 0.3g   Threonine 1.4g   Isoleucine 1.6g
Leucine 2.7g   Lysine 2.5g   Methionine 0.5g
Cystine 0.5g   Glycine 1.6g   Serine 1.9g
Glutamic acid 6.7g   Valine 1.6g   Arginine 3.6g
Aspartic acid 4.5g   Alanine 1.6g   Proline 1.5g
Phenylalanine 2.0g   Histidine 1.0g   Tyrosine 0.9g

Great Northern Beans

Great Northern Beans are very high in both protein and fiber, along with potassium, selenium, and all of the eight essential amino acids.

One cup of Great Northern Beans contains the following:

Protein 40.0g   **Carbohydrate** 114.1g
Fiber 36.9g   **Ash** 7.1g

Minerals:
Calcium 320.2mg   Iron 10.0mg
Magnesium 345.8mg   Phosphorus 818.0mg
Potassium 2538.2mg   Sodium 25.6mg
Zinc 4.2mg   Copper 1.5mg
Manganese 2.6mg   Selenium 23.6mcg

Vitamins:
Thiamin 1.1mg   Riboflavin 0.4mg
Niacin 3.5mg   Pantothenic acid 2.0mg
Vit. B-6 0.8mg   Folate 882.0mcg
Vit. A 5.4 IU   Vit. C 9.6mg

Amino acids:
Tryptophan 0.4g   Threonine 1.6g   Isoleucine 1.7g
Leucine 3.1g   Lysine 2.7g   Methionine 0.6g
Cystine 0.4g   Tyrosine 1.1g   Valine 2.0g
Phenylalanine 2.1g   Histidine 1.1g   Alanine 1.6g
Glutamic acid 6.0g   Serine 2.1g   Proline 1.6g
Aspartic acid 4.8g   Glycine 1.5g   Arginine 2.4g

Kidney Beans

One cup of Kidney beans (all types) contain the following:

Protein 43.3g   **Carbohydrate** 110.4g
Fiber 45.8g   **Ash** 7.0g

Minerals:
Calcium 263.1mg   Iron 15.0mg
Magnesium 257.6mg   Phosphorus 748.8mg
Potassium 2587.0 mg   Sodium 44.1mg
Zinc 5.1mg   Copper 1.7mg
Manganese 1.8mg   Selenium 5.8mcg

Vitamins:
Thiamin 0.9mg   Riboflavin 0.4mg
Niacin 3.7mg   Pantothenic acid 1.4mg
Vit B-6 0.7mg   Folate 724.9mcg
Vit. A 14.7 IU   Vit. C 8.2mg

Amino acids:
Tryptophan 0.5g   Threonine 1.8g   Isoleucine 1.9g
Leucine 3.4g   Lysine 2.9g   Methionine 0.6g
Cystine 0.6g   Proline 1.8g   Serine 2.3g
Glutamic acid 6.6g   Valine 2.2g   Arginine 2.6g
Phenylalanine 2.3g   Alanine 1.8g   Glycine 1.6g
Aspartic acid 5.2g   Tyrosine 1.2g   Histidine 1.2g

Soybeans

Soybeans are one of the best beans to add to your food storage. They can be made into flour, milk, tofu, and they can be sprouted. Soybeans and peanuts are made up of the most complete protein of the legumes.

One cup of Soybeans contains the following:

Protein 67.8g   **Carbohydrate** 56.0g
Fiber 17.2g   **Ash** 9.0g

Minerals:
Calcium 515.2mg   Iron 29.2mg
Magnesium 520.8mg   Phosphorus 1309.mg
Potassium 3342.4mg   Sodium 3.7mg
Zinc 9.0mg   Copper 3.0mg
Manganese 4.6mg   Selenium 33.1mcg

Vitamins:
Thiamin 1.6mg   Riboflavin 1.6mg
Niacin 3.0mg   Pantothenic acid 1.4mg
Vit. B-6 0.7mg   Folate 697.5mcg
Vit. E 3.6mg_ATE   Vit. A 44.6 IU
Vit. C 11.1mg   Tocopherol, alpha 1.5mg

Amino acids:
Tryptophan 0.9g   Threonine 2.9g   Isoleucine 3.2g
Leucine 5.5g   Lysine 4.5g   Methionine 0.9g
Phenylalanine 3.5g   Cystine 1.0g   Tyrosine 2.5g
Aspartic acid 8.5g   Valine 3.3g   Arginine 5.2g
Histidine 1.8g   Alanine 3.1g   Glycine 3.1g
Glutamic acid 13.1g Proline 3.9g   Serine 3.9g

Mung Beans

Mung beans are excellent for sprouting. Mung beans are sprouted under pressure in order to create large juicy sprouts.

One cup of Mung beans contains the following:

Protein 49.3   **Carbohydrate** 129.6g
Fiber 33.7g   **Ash** 0.4g

Minerals:
Calcium 273.2mg   Iron 13.9mg
Magnesium 391.2mg   Phosphorus 759.6mg
Potassium 2579.2mg   Sodium 31.0mg
Zinc 5.5mg   Copper 1.9mg
Manganese 2.1mg   Selenium 16.9mcg

Vitamins:
Thiamin 1.2mg   Riboflavin 0.4mg
Niacin 4.6mg   Pantothenic acid 3.9mg
Vit. B-6 0.7mg   Folate 1293.7mcg
Vit. E 1.0mg_ATE   Vit. A 235.9 IU
Vit. C 9.9mg

Amino acids:
Tryptophan 0.5g   Threonine 1.6g   Isoleucine 2.0g
Leucine 3.8g   Lysine 3.4g   Methionine 0.5g
Phenylalanine 2.9g   Cystine 0.4g   Tyrosine 1.4g
Glutamic acid 8.8g   Valine 2.5g   Arginine 3.4g
Histidine 1.4g   Alanine 2.1g   Serine 2.4g
Aspartic acid 5.7g   Glycine 1.9g   Proline 2.2g

Split Peas

Split peas can not be sprouted, only whole peas are able to sprout. Split peas are mostly used for split pea soup.

One cup of Split Peas contains the following:

Protein 48.3   **Carbohydrate** 118.9g
Fiber 50.2g   **Ash** 5.2g

Minerals:

Calcium 108.3mg	Iron 8.7mg
Magnesium 226.5mg	Phosphorus 721.0mg
Potassium 1932.5mg	Sodium 29.5mg
Zinc 5.9mg	Copper 1.7mg
Manganese 2.7mg	Selenium 3.1mcg

Vitamins:

Thiamin 1.4mg	Riboflavin 0.4mg
Niacin 5.6mg	Pantothenic acid 3.4mg
Vit. B-6 0.3mg	Folate 539.7mcg
Vit. E 0.5mg_ATE	Vit. A 293.5 IU
Vit. C 3.5mg	Tocopherol, alpha 0.7mg

Amino acids:

Tryptophan 0.5g	Threonine 1.7g	Isoleucine 1.9g
Leucine 3.4g	Lysine 3.4g	Methionine 0.4g
Cystine 0.7g	Tyrosine 1.4g	Valine 2.2g
Phenylalanine 2.2g	Arginine 4.3g	Histidine 1.1g
Glutamic acid 8.2g	Alanine 2.1g	Glycine 2.1g
Aspartic acid 5.7g	Proline 1.9g	Serine 2.1g

Seeds

Seeds

Seeds are the potential for life and are a highly concentrated food source. When seeds are sprouted they reach their highest nutritional value in as short as one to three days. They contain all the nutritional elements to start new life.

Seeds can be ground and used as spices and flavorings, such as celery seeds, cumin, mustard, cardamom, coriander as well as many others.

Seeds are also used to produce oils such as sesame oil, sunflower oil, flaxseed oil and others. Many, such as pumpkin seeds are rich in protein and high in minerals and vitamins.

Seeds are a powerhouse full of nutrition. If utilized to the fullest we could sustain life for a long period of time.

With seeds you have the ability to grow your own fresh live produce. Have you ever thought what you would do if there were no fresh produce in the stores and it was winter? Well sprouting is your answer. It does not take large quantities to nourish our bodies, and it is easy to do. For the amount of sprouts produced from the seeds, this becomes one of the lowest cost food items to purchase.

Sprouting saves time, they are high in nutritional value, they save you money compared to fresh produce at the store, and you can always have fresh live food available, we have no excuse but to keep sprouts going all the time and have plenty of seeds in our storage.

Flaxseed

Flaxseeds help digestion; you can boil them to make a flaxseed tea. Flaxseed in my opinion is a must. It is easy to mill in a small grain (coffee) grinder and added to cereals, smoothies, etc. Flax seed should be added to everything.

Flax seed is high in Omega 3 fatty acids. Flax also contains a plant fiber called Lignan that help protects us from most devastating diseases including, heart disease, cancer and stroke. Lignans are amazing nutrients that have antibacterial and anti-viral properties.

The National Cancer Institute found that Flax seed did indeed have an anti-cancer effect. Information in "Flax for Life" by Jade Beutler & Ann Louise Gittleman

One cup of Flaxseeds contains the following:

Protein 30.2   **Carbohydrate** 53.0g
Fiber 43.2g   **Ash** 5.4g

Minerals:
Calcium 308.4mg   Iron 9.6mg
Magnesium 561.1mg   Phosphorus 771.9mg
Potassium 1055.5mg   Sodium 52.7mg
Zinc 6.4mg   Copper 1.6mg
Manganese 5.0mg   Selenium 8.5mcg

Vitamins:
Thiamin 0.2mg   Riboflavin 0.2mg
Niacin 2.1mg   Pantothenic acid 2.3mg
Vit. B-6 1.4mg   Folate 430.9mcg
Vit. E 7.7mg_ATE

Pumpkin and Squash Seeds

High in Omega 6's pumpkin seeds may be blended with water to make a nutritious nut milk to add creaminess to soups and sauces. Whole they can be eaten raw or added to salads, grain dishes, trail mixes, stir fry, casseroles and cookies. When pumpkin seeds are milled they can be added to almost anything.

Pumpkin seeds have been excepted as an effective vermicide, as such they are used in the treatment of intestinal worms, and in the treatment and prevention of prostrate problems.

Pumpkin and squash seeds are very similar in their nutriational content. They are best known for their zinc content and they are very high in protein. Pumpkin seeds also contain essential fatty acids and vitamin E. They contain a good balance of amino acids, calcium, iron, vitamin A and B vitamins.

One cup of Pumpkin seeds contains the following:

Protein 33.8   **Carbohydrate** 24.5g
Fiber 5.3g   **Ash** 6.7g

Minerals:

Calcium 59.3mg   Iron 20.6mg
Magnesium 738.3mg   Phosphorus 1620.1mg
Potassium 1113.6mg   Sodium 24.8mg
Zinc 10.2mg   Copper 1.9mg
Manganese 4.1mg   Selenium 7.7mcg

Vitamins:

Thiamin 0.2mg

Niacin 2.4mg

Pantothenic acid 0.4mg

Folate 80.0mcg

Vit. C 2.6mg

Riboflavin 0.4mg

Vit. A 524.4 IU

Vit. B-6 0.3mg

Vit. E 1.3mg_ATE

Amino acids:

Tryptophan 0.5g

Leucine 2.8g

Cystine 0.4g

Phenylalanine 1.6g

Aspartic acid 3.4g

Glutamic acid 5.9g

Threonine 1.2g

Lysine 2.5g

Valine 2.7g

Glycine 2.4g

Tyrosine 1.4g

Alanine 1.5g

Isoleucine 1.7g

Methionine 0.7g

Arginine 5.5g

Proline 1.3g

Histidine 0.9g

Serine 1.5g

Alfalfa Seeds

Alfalfa seeds are by far the most common seeds used for sprouting. They contain A, C, E, K, and B vitamins. They also contain Calcium, Magnesium, Potassium, Zinc, Iron and Selenium.

Broccoli Sprouting Seeds

Broccoli sprouting seeds are scientifically proven to help fight cancer, and these sprouts are ready in 5-6 days. They contain a wide variety of Vitamins, Minerals, and Amino Acids.

Cabbage Seeds

Cabbage seeds when sprouted contain vitamins A, C, and U. They also contain many trace elements including iodine and sulfur. Cabbage is one of the most nutritious vegetable sprouts and are used at some cancer clinics.

Fenugreek Seeds

Fenugreek seeds when sprouted acts as a blood and kidney cleanser. Along with being a power house full of nutrients, and trace elements.

Sesame Seeds

Sesame Seeds are very high in mineral content along with most of the B vitamins, except B-12 and folic acid. They are also rich in protein, Vitamin E and fiber. Milk made from sesame seeds that have been sprouted one to two days, have almost as much calcium as cow's milk. Zinc as well as magnesium, potassium, and phosphorus is also high in sesame seeds. Because of the high phosphorus to calcium ratio it does not allow for maximum bone support.

Sunflower Seeds

Sunflower seeds are very high in potassium and extremely low in sodium, as such they have been helpful to people with high blood pressure and cardiovascular problems.

They are also used for increased energy. Sprouted Sun-flower seeds are one of the riches edible seeds. Sunflower seeds are a good source of the Vitamin B complex, also Vitamin E, Fats and Protein. They are very high in Mineral content. Pumpkin, Sesame, and Sunflower seeds are nearly twenty to thirty percent protein.

There are many other seed to consider many are mentioned in chapter 14. Most all seeds are highly packed with nutrition which is vital to our health. We need the live enzymes provided to us by living seeds, plants, and grasses.

Nuts

Nuts
The Choices are Yours

Nuts should become a part of your food storage. You will want to get fresh nuts. Nuts store longer when stored in their shells. This keeps the nuts fresher and in most cases keeps the oxygen away from the meat of the nut. If you choose to buy and store shelled nuts, they are better kept in the refrigerator or freezer to keep the oils in the nuts from going rancid.

Nut milks are easy to digest, nutritious, and delicious. They are also easy to make. Take approximately one ounce of nuts with one or two cups of distilled water, depending on the consistency you like. Then put in your electric blender half the water, nuts and sweetener then blend. Add the additional water as desired. If you soak your nuts over night you will have a creamery substance. You can then strain the pulp or drink it as is. You can use the pulp in soups, grains or in meat dishes. You can also buy a soymilk processor and have the whole process completed in twelve minutes.

Nuts when added to meat dishes aids in digestion. They can be chopped and added to grain dishes, soups, and salads, or left whole and be eaten plain or added to trail mixes.

Nuts that are recommended for your health are: Almonds, Brazil Nuts, Hazelnuts, Pistachios (avoid the salty and the red-dyed nuts), and Walnuts.

Almonds

Almonds are alkaline, you can enjoy them raw or soaked for easy digestion. Almonds can also be  made into a delicious milk. Almonds are not actually sprouted they are soaked ten to twelve hours, they will plump up as they swell with water. Almonds will add a whole new dimension of enzymes, which are necessary for many of our body functions. Almonds are one of the best nuts to add to your diet and food storage. They make an excellent almond milk. Almonds contain amygdalin, known as lactrile which has caused them to be used in diets for cancer prevention and are used in cancer clinics.

One cup of whole Almonds contains the following:

Protein 30.1   **Carbohydrate** 28.3g
Fiber 16.7g   **Ash** 4.4g

Minerals:
Calcium 352.1mg   Iron 6.1mg
Magnesium 390.5mg   Phosphorus 673.0mg
Potassium 1033.7mg   Sodium 1.4mg
Zinc 4.7mg   Copper 1.5mg
Manganese 3.6mg   Selenium 6.2mcg

Vitamins:
Thiamin 0.3mg   Riboflavin 1.1mg
Niacin 5.5mg   Pantothenic acid 0.4mg
Vit. B-6 0.1mg   Folate 41.1mcg

Vit. E 37.7mg_ATE
Tocopherol, alpha 36.7mg
Tocopherol, gamma 1.2mg

Vit. A 14.2 IU
Tocopherol, beta 0.6mg
Tocopherol, delta 3.6mg

Amino acids:

Tryptophan 0.2g	Threonine 0.9g	Isoleucine 0.9g
Leucine 2.8g	Lysine 0.8g	Methionine 0.2g
Cystine 0.4g	Tyrosine 0.7g	Valine 1.1g
Phenylalanine 1.6g	Proline 1.3g	Serine 1.4g
Aspartic acid 3.8g	Arginine 3.5g	Histidine 0.8g
Glutamic acid 7.3g	Glycine 2.0g	Alanine 1.4g

Peanuts, all types raw

Peanuts are not really nuts, they are of the legume family. They have a good balance of amino acids as they are a bean. Some of the people who show a sensitivity towards peanuts, are really sensitive to the molds not the peanut itself. Stored peanuts may easily become moldy. Peanuts have been known to become contaminated with molds that contain aflatoxin which maybe a cancer causing substance. Along with that, processed peanut butters usually have hydrogenated fats added, which are added toxins to the body along with other additives. Processed peanut butter is not the best choice for health. It is best to grind your own peanuts for peanut butter. You now see more stores that allow you to grind your own fresh peanut butter. You should store peanut butter in the refrigerator to prevent the oils from becoming rancid. Some people find they have digestive problems with peanuts and people that have gallbladder problems find they can not tolerate them. Peanuts should be consumed in moderation.

Peanuts and Soybeans are the most complete proteins of the legumes. Peanuts provide a good source of fiber and minerals.

One cup of raw Peanuts contains the following:

Protein 37.6   **Carbohydrate** 23.5g

Fiber 12.4g   **Ash** 3.4g

Minerals:

Calcium 134.3mg

Magnesium 245.2mg

Potassium 1029.3mg

Zinc 4.7mg

Manganese 2.8mg

Iron 6.6mg

Phosphorus 548.9mg

Sodium 26.2mg

Copper 1.6mg

Selenium 10.5mcg

Vitamins:

Thiamin 0.9mg

Niacin 17.6mg

Vit. B-6 0.5mg

Tocopherol, alpha 12.1mg

Riboflavin 0.1mg

Pantothenic acid 2.5mg

Folate 350.4mcg

Vit. E 13.3mg_ATE

Amino acids:

Tryptophan 0.3g

Leucine 2.4g

Phenylalanine 1.9g

Aspartic acid 4.5g

Histidine 0.9g

Glutamic acid 7.8g

Threonine 1.2g

Lysine 1.3g

Cystine 0.4g

Valine 1.5g

Alanine 1.4g

Glycine 2.2g

Isoleucine 1.3g

Methionine 0.4g

Tyrosine 1.5g

Arginine 4.5g

Serine 1.8g

Proline 1.63g

Sweeteners

Honey

Honey contains trace enzymes, minerals, vitamins, and amino acids. Honey is also rated with the highest energy factor of all sweeteners.

Honey should not be given to a child under the age of one year, because it may contain bacterial spores which has caused infant botulism. It is rare but a serious disease that effects the nervous system of young babies. "The safety of Honey as a food for older children and adults remains unquestioned". (Center for Disease Control).

Honey should be stored in sterile glass jars. If the lid is not enamel, put plastic wrap over the filled jar and seal tightly. This is the same for all liquid sweeteners.

One cup of strained or extracted honey contains the following:

Minerals:

Calcium 20.3mg	Iron 1.4mg	Magnesium 6.7mg
Phosphorus 13.5mg	Zinc 0.7mg	Sodium 13.5mg
Copper 0.1mg	Potassium 176mg	
Manganese 0.3mg	Selenium 2.7mcg	

Vitamins:

Thiamin 0mg	Riboflavin 0.1mg
Niacin 0.4mg	Pantothenic acid 0.2mg
Vit. B-6 0.08mg	Folate 6.7mcg

Amino acids:

Tryptophan 0.01g

Isoleucine 0.02g

Lysine 0.02g

Cystine 0.01g

Tyrosine 0.02g

Arginine 0.01g

Alanine 0.2g

Glutamine acid 0.06g

Proline 0.3g

Threonine 0.01g

Leucine 0.03g

Methionine 0.003g

Phenylalanine 0.03g

Valine 0.3g

Histidine 0.003g

Aspartic acid 0.09g

Glycine 0.02g

Serine 0.02g

Barley Syrup

Barley syrup is made from whole barley grain that has been sprouted. Barley syrup is very mild.

Brown Rice Syrup

Brown Rice syrup is made from brown rice and whole barley. This syrup has a very mild taste.

Molasses

Blackstrap molasses is high in trace minerals and iron. It has a strong flavor and is not very sweet. Molasses is a by product of refined white, and brown sugar. Blackstrap molasses is exceptionally high in the calcium to phosphorus ratio and does support your bones. It is also very high in selenium, potassium, and other minerals. This is an excellent choice to add to your storage.

You can also buy sweet or light molasses, it does not contain the nutrients that blackstrap molasses does.

Molasses should be stored in sterile glass jars. If the lid is not enamel, put plastic wrap over the filled jar and seal tightly. This is the same for all liquid sweeteners.

One cup Blackstrap Molasses contains the following:

Ash 10.8g

Minerals:

Calcium 672.4mg

Phosphorus 101.6mg

Sodium 121.3mg

Zinc 0.9mg

Manganese 5.0mg

Iron 15.4mg

Potassium 4801.9mg

Magnesium 793.7mg

Copper 1.5mg

Selenium 58.3

Vitamins:

Thiamin 0.1mg

Niacin 3.0mg

Vitamin B-6 2.1mg

Riboflavin 0.0mg

Pantothenic acid 2.6mg

Sorghum

Sorghum is high in trace minerals, amino acids, and is mild tasting.

Sorghum should be stored in sterile glass jars. If the lid is not enamel, put plastic wrap over the filled jar and seal tightly. This is the same for all liquid sweeteners.

One cup of strained or extracted sorghum contains the following:

Ash 3.0g

Minerals:
Calcium 53.7mg   Iron 8.4mg
Phosphorus 551.0mg   Potassium 672.0mg
Sodium 11.5mg

Vitamins:
Thiamin 0.4mg   Riboflavin 0.2mg   Niacin 5.6mg

Amino acids:
Tryptophan 0.2g	Threonine 0.6g	Isoleucine 0.8g
Leucine 2.8g	Lysine 0.4g	Methionine 0.3g
Cystine 0.2g	Arginine 0.6g	Histidine 0.4g
Phenylalanine 1.0g	Proline 1.6g	Serine 0.8g
Tyrosine 0.6g	Valine 1.0g	Alanine 1.9g
Aspartic acid 1.4g	Glycine 0.6g	
Glutamine acid 4.6g		

Fructose

Fructose is the sugar found in fruit. This is dried and can be used as a replacement for white sugar.

Refined White Sugar

Refined white sugar is not good for the body and should not be your only source or choice of sweetener.

White sugar should be stored knowing that there is very little nutrient value.

One cup of sugar contains the following:

Minerals:

Calcium 2.0mg   Iron 0.1mg
Phosphorus 4.0mg   Potassium 4.0mg
Sodium 2.0mg   Zinc 0.06mg
Copper 0.08mg   Manganese 0.01mg
Selenium 1.2mcg

Vitamins:
Riboflavin 0.006mg

Powdered Sugar

Powder sugar has even less nutrients than refined white sugar and is not recommended for your health. If you choose to store powder sugar it should be stored in the original package and then put in an airtight container.

One cup of powdered sugar contains the following:

Minerals:

Calcium 1.2mg   Iron 0.07mg
Potassium 2.4mg   Sodium 1.2mg
Copper 0.05mg   Manganese 0.008mg
Selenium 0.7mcg   Phosphorus 2.4mg
Zinc 0.03mg

Brown Sugar

Brown sugar should be stored in the same way honey is due to the high moisture content.

One cup of brown sugar contains the following:

Ash 1.9g

Minerals:

Calcium 187.0mg	Magnesium 63.8mg
Phosphorus 48.4mg	Zinc 0.3mg
Potassium 761.2mg	Sodium 85.8mg
Copper 0.6mg	Manganese 0.7mg
Selenium 2.6mcg	Iron 4.2mg

Vitamins:

Thiamin 0.01mg	Riboflavin 0.01mg
Niacin 0.1mg	Pantothenic acid 0.2mg
Vit. B-6 0.05mg	Folate 2.2mcg

Stevia (Stevioside)

With all the data made available today regarding refined sugar and artificial sweeteners it is indeed a blessing to have had bestowed upon us a spectacular item the likes of Steviocide.

Stevia is an extraordinarily sweet herb. Generally speaking this is the answer for anyone suffering from any type of blood sugar disorder, candidiasis, chronic fatigue, cancers, HIV, AIDS, etc. where any type of sugar works against the body in overcoming these conditions. Stevia helps to neutralizes an acidic environment, preventing a pH imbalance due to an over ingestion of sugar or carbohydrate intake.

Stevia enhances the taste of any other sweetener. A pinch of Stevia used with any other sweetener cuts down tremendously on the amount of the other sweet products that need to be used, there by reducing the sugar grams taken into the body.

Stevia is almost calorie free. Unlike sugar, it does not trigger a raise in blood sugar and yet it increases energy and aids digestion by stimulating the pancreas.

Stevia is available in several forms, including a green powder and a brownish liquid extract, which has a strong, licorice-like taste. I use the white powder. It comes in two strengths. One is 55% extract of steviocide crystals the other is 85-95%.

To make your own liquid for sweetener, take 1tsp. 95%

white stevia extract (actually the white powder) and combine it with 3 tablespoons of filtered or distilled water. Store in the refrigerator in a dropper type container until ready to use. It only takes a few drops to sweeten most beverages. One teaspoon of Stevia powder is equal to one cup of sugar.

Oils

Oils
The Choices are Yours

Essential Fatty Acids

Fatty Acids, which the body is unable to manufacture on its own, must be supplied through food sources. These are called Essential Fatty Acids. These have a multitude of benefits and everyone needs to obtain these through healthy sources. Essential fatty acids are known to reduce cholesterol and blood pressure and reduce the risk of heart disease and stroke.

Essential fatty acids help to prevent tumors, fibroids, and cysts. Being that the brain is primarily made up of fatty tissue, these essential fats feed and protect the brain's capacity for health and proper functioning. "Good" fats in the diet promote healthy skin and lubrication for joints.

Essential fatty acids function as building blocks in the membranes of each and every cell. Also, they produce "prostaglandin families". These short acting hormone-like substances are necessary for cell to cell biochemical functions, such as energy metabolism, cardiovascular and immune health.

Healing Fats: *A closer look at essential fatty acids by UDO Erasmus, Ph. D., Internationally recognized Essential Fatty Acid Authority and Author "Fats That Heal, Fats That Kill"*

Like minerals, the body cannot make essential fatty acids, yet the body absolutely requires these healing fats. Essential fatty acids have been more neglected than any other essential nutrient.

There are two essential fatty acids that the body cannot synthesize and must consume from dietary sources. These are the omega-3 and omega-6 fatty acids. Omega-3 fatty acids are needed to produce elcosapentaenoic acid (EPA) and docsahexaenoic acid (DHA). Omega-6 fatty acids, also known as linoleic acids are found in many vegetable oils, most notably evening primrose oil. Omega-6 fatty acids are the parent substance for an important substance called gammalinolenic acid (GLA).

The body uses omega-6 fatty acids to metabolize another important substance called GLA. In turn, GLA is used to create prostaglandin, a hormone-like substances that regulate many of the body functions. The conversion of omega-6 to GLA is a tricky business. Many substances can interfere, such as alcohol, tobacco, increasing age, stress, illness, and other dietary fats, and low levels of vitamins and minerals.

It also seems that during the inflammatory process of rheumatoid arthritis, the body is producing too much of the "wrong" prostaglandin and not enough of the "right" kind. GLA helps the body produce the prostaglandin that reduces inflammation.

Minor ingredients found in minimally processed oils, such oils-soluble phytochemicals, are also very valuable to health. Lignans and other minor ingredients are called impurities by some industries, but some health conscious manufactures call them minor ingredients and realize that they have a major effect on health. Their positive health benefits include antioxidant activity, cardiovascular protection, and maintenance of healthy skin, anti-microbial activity, and tumor inhibition.

Misconceptions: Fats and oils are sorely misunderstood.

There is a big advertising scam that polyunsaturated fats made from partially hydrogenated fats are beneficial to the heart, but the real truth is partially hydrogenated fats are detrimental to health.

Misinformation disseminated to Americans is the message that some fats are okay for frying. All fried fats hurt the heart. A healthy diet should provide 15-20% of calories from fat and a portion of this should be essential fatty acids.

Essential fatty acids play a variety of roles toward a healthy body. The most basic of these is in energy production. Athletes may find that essential fatty acids increase their stamina and performance while reducing their recovery time.

Another very important function of essential fatty acids is in neural development. Omega-3 fatty acids enhance visual function in infants. New research shows that expectant mothers supplementing with omega-3 fatty acids give birth to infants with higher levels of essential fatty acids.

An interesting quality to essential fatty acids is that they provide energy, but at the same time are calming. This may explain why essential fatty acids are purported to treat ADHD and hyper-activity.

Essential fatty acids are also said to elevate the mood and lift depression. Other healthy roles of essential fatty acids are in the maintenance of the cardiovascular system and immune system, proper insulin function, and inhibit tumor growth.

Deficiencies of essential fatty acids manifest as eczema, hair loss, compromised immune function, reproductive problems, behavioral changes, growth retardation, increased blood pressure, and elevated triglyceride levels.

A test for determining if one's diet provides adequate amounts of essential fatty acids is by simply feeling the skin. If it is soft, smooth and velvety, the person has adequate essential fatty acid intake. The test works because the brain, liver, and other organs have priority for essential fatty acids. The skin is last in line. So if the skin is healthy, the body as a whole has adequate levels of essential fatty acids.

Storing Fats and Oils

Fats and Oils should be kept closed in bottles to prevent deterioration by air and light. Store in a cool (50 to 70 degrees F) dry place. Minimize time of exposure to light since it can accelerate rancidity development.

You should store all oils in the size of containers that your family would consume within a month or two. Opened oils will go rancid if not used in a timely manner.

Light, heat, and exposure to oxygen in the air will affect the storage life. Vegetable oils and solid shortenings stored in the dark, with original packaging seal unbroken, at temperatures below 75 degrees F will generally keep one or two years with out noticeable change (some brands or types taste different than others to start with). If they are kept at 60 degrees F they will keep twice as long (assuming they are not in a can which rusts out).

Mayonnaise and salad dressing are usually dated and will store about a year if keep cool (below 75 degrees F), in the dark, and in the original sealed container. These are not the best oils for your body, unless you are making your own dressings with good oils.

Flax Seed Oil
A Nutritionally Superior Oil

The oil from fresh flaxseed contains many favorable health benefits. That's because flaxseed Oil is one of nature's riches sources of Omega-3 fatty acids now considered essential for maintaining good health. Its flavor is wholesome and nutty. In order to preserve its superior nutritional value unrefined flaxseed Oil should not be used in cooking but rather in cold food preparations such as salad dressings or dips. Maximum benefits are derived when combined with a sulfur containing protein such as garlic, onions or soymilk.

Flaxseed oil contains an average of 57% Omega-3 EFA (essential fatty acids), 16% Omega-6 EFA, and 18% of the highly beneficial non-essential Omega-9 FA. Flaxseed oil is naturally high in the antioxidant nutrients Beta-Carotene (4300 IU/Tbsp.) and Vitamin E (15 IU/Tbsp.).

Brazilnut oil

Brazilnut oil is high in monounsaturates making it suitable for cooking. This oil has a delightful nutty flavor.

Canola Oil
Canola (meaning Canadian Oil)

Canola oil is known as "low erucic acid rapeseed oil" and is the result of years of selective plant breeding in Canada. Unrefined Canola oil has a rich, golden color and a strong savory flavor. It is not recommended for cooking due to its omega-3 content. It is best used in salad dressings and mayonnaise or directly on grains or vegetables.

Hazelnut Oil

Hazelnut oil has a delicate flavor and bouquet. Many Gold Medal Chefs consider hazelnut the finest gourmet oil; it is excellent on salads and pasta and marvelous in pancakes and muffins. By adding this exquisite oil to simple food, such as tortellini or baked squash, you can make the ordinary extraordinary. Hazelnut oil is high in monounsaturates making it suitable for cooking.

Olive Oil

Fresh Olive Oil has an aromatic bouquet and imparts a "Mediterranean" flavor to even ordinary recipes. It is ideal for sautéing and delicious in salad dressings and spreads. Olive oil is the most versatile cooking oil. Extra Virgin and Virgin cold pressed are the only varieties guaranteed to be unrefined. Extra Virgin is made from the first pressing and has an acid level of less than 1%; with continued pressing, the acidity rises.

Pumpkin Seed Oil

Pumpkin oil is suitable for sautéing. Pumpkin oil has a delightful flavor and a stunning color it also adds pizzazz to salad dressings, vegetables, and pasta dishes.

Safflower Oil

In its unrefined form, Safflower Oil has a wonderful flavor. Probably the most versatile of all vegetable oils, it can be used for sautéing and baking, as well as in dressings, sauces, dips and mayonnaise. It is especially delicious in grain salads.

Sesame Oil

The sesame seed is a nutritional staple in the Middle East. It also provides the familiar Sesame flavor in traditional oriental stir-fry and macrobiotic cooking. Sesame Oil contains sesames a natural preservative, making the oil very stable and suitable for all cooking needs.

Sunflower Oil

The Sunflower's origins are in South America. The Incas used Sunflower Oil in diverse ways. It adds the fresh taste of sunflower seeds to green salads, dressings, sauces, and baked goods.

Coconut Butter

This non-hydrogenated naturally saturated oil contains no transfatty acids (TFAs) and is solid at room temperature (below 24 degrees C and 76 degrees F). It is ideal for cooking and is the perfect vegan/dairy-free alternative to butter. When unprocessed, naturally saturated coconut oil is part of a healthy diet. There is usually no change in serum cholesterol levels. For example, researchers have noted that the Polynesians and the Bicolanos (of the Philippines) include coconut oil in their daily diets and have low serum cholesterol levels and little coronary disease.

Do not be scared by the fact that coconut oil is naturally saturated: current research shows it is no longer correct to think that all saturated fatty acids raise cholesterol. There are two groups of saturated fats, medium and long chain. Each acts differently in your body. Long chain saturates store as fats and are associated with "bad" cholesterol. Medium chain saturates, found in coconut oil, do not clog arteries nor do they cause heart disease. Instead, a medium chain saturates digest easily and are an excellent source of fuel and energy.

Because coconut oil is naturally saturated, it does not need to be hydrogenated. This process causes fat to change from liquid to solid at room temperature and is used in manufacturing of most margarines and shortenings. The result of hydrogenation is a poisonous molecular distortion of the fatty acids, turning them into harmful trans fats (TFAs). Researchers have pointed out these warped fatty acids raise "bad" cholesterol (LDL) and lower "good" cholesterol

(HDL) levels.

You should not consume hydrogenated or partially hydrogenated oils, in any form or in any ingredient.

Essential Balance TM

Essential Balance TM is the only organic oil blend using the combination of unrefined Flax, Sunflower, Sesame, Pumpkin, and Borage oils. Together these organic oils taste uniquely rich and nutty. It contains a healthy 1:1 ratio of omega-6 to omega-3. This special blend also offers gamma-linolenic acid (GLA), a derivative of omega-6. (Information furnished by Omega Nutrition, makers of Omegaflo Healthy Oils).

Sprouting

Sprouting
How and Why to use some of your
Grains, Beans, and Lentils

Genesis 1:29
And God said, Behold, I have given you every herb bearing
seed, which is upon the face of all the earth, and every
tree, in the which is the fruit of a tree yielding seed; to you it
shall be for meat.

Sprouts are live plants. They are one of the best foods you can eat. Sprouts have the minerals, vitamins, protein, and enzymes that our bodies thrive on in order to be healthy. Sprouts are alkaline, and help to balance our bodies. They provide a good source of fiber.

Everyone must learn to sprout the grains and beans that you store and incorporate them in your meals and munch on them as snacks. Sprouting is the easiest garden you can have and the least time consuming. You can have sprouts in as little as one to five days depending on the grain, seed, nut, or bean and they can be grown indoors in any climate.

Use organic or untreated seeds. Do not use seeds that are treated for agriculture use.

Sprouts come close to being a perfect food. Sprouts are live foods. They contain live enzymes necessary for digestion and proper assimilation of food nutrients. Sprouts are a high source of natural fiber.

Never has nutrition been as important as it is today. Our modern day diets and commercial processing of our foods have left us a nation of people filled with empty calories, preservatives, and all kinds of additives. Now you can grow fresh, live, wholesome sprouts packed with all the natural vitamins, nutrients, and enzymes God and nature intended you to have. Fresh sprouted seeds increase an amazing 30%-600% in some vitamins, minerals, and protein content. Sprouts are some of the most nutritious foods available.

As seeds begin to sprout, nutritional value multiplies in almost all areas. According to a study by the renowned biochemist Dr. Jeffrey Bland, the B complex content in germinated wheat increases 600 percent in the first 72 hours. Vitamin E content is tripled and Vitamin C increases six-fold. Sprouts are also higher in minerals than their ungerminated counterparts but are generally low in sodium and are low in carbohydrates. Sprouts are high in protein as the following list shows.

Protein Content
Eggs   13%
Meat   19%
Mung bean sprouts   24%
Lentils 25%
Soy sprouts   28%
Alfalfa sprouts   35% ...according to *Back to Basics*

Sprouting is one of the fastest ways of improving the nutritional value of the grains and beans you have stored. There are more nutrients in a seed after it has germinated than at any other time of its life cycle. This is because of the amount of nutrients released to aid the seed in its growing process. As with wheat after it has sprouted there develops additional nutrients than it had before.

Using sprouts can take the place of fresh vegetables. You can utilize them in almost every facet of your cooking. You can use them as snacks, in salads, stir-fry, in juices, add them to soup, rice, steamed vegetables, casseroles, omelets, sandwiches, meat loaf, and baked goods.

Remember these are live foods. To ensure the least amount of nutritional lost add sprouts at the very end of cooking. If adding to yeast breads make sure you add them as late as possible to the dough. They have live enzymes and can start to digest the proteins and inhibit the yeast. This could make a very heavy loaf of bread or the dough could sour if it is left to sit too long.

Precautions:

- Don't sprout seeds treated for agricultural use – they are generally treated with poisonous insecticides and are not safe for human consumption.

Soybean sprouts contain the following:
Isoflavones, (plant estrogens) that help prevent hormone-dependent cancers.
Genistein, an enzyme that can inhibit tumor growth.
Protease inhibitors, may prevent or inhibit a wide range of cancers.
Physic acid, a plant compound that may reduce the size and number of tumors.
Saponins (also found in chickpeas and ginseng) have been shown in animal studies to lower the risk of certain cancers.

Basic Sprouting

Selecting Seeds

Select good seeds, grains, or beans for sprouting. Look for uniformity of shape, make sure the seeds are not broken or chipped. This may lead to souring or rotting of the sprouts. Organic, pesticide free seeds are preferred.

Basic Care

The main focus with sprouting is to keep the sprout moist, while maintaining good drainage and good air circulation. If sprouts are not rinsed and drained properly they will sour. The more consistent you are with regular rinsing the healthier they will be.

Sprouts like to be warm around 70 degrees. If you are sprouting in an area that is cold you can help by rinsing with warm water, and insulating a cardboard box to set your sprouting jars or trays in. Remember they also need good circulating air. If the area is rather hot, rinse with cold water.

Soaking

Most all Sprouting starts the same way. Take the seeds and soak them in hot tap water. The 130 to 160 degree water wakes up the germ faster and gets it growing. Don't worry about the water being too hot to kill that germ because it does not hurt the germ at the beginning point, it gets the seed started faster. This is the only time you would use hot water.

When soaking the seeds if pests are visible discard all of the seeds from that batch, not just the ones you were soaking.

Drain

Drain and rinse the seeds. If the seeds are not drained completely they will sour. If you are using trays make sure you tip them to the corner and drain out all the water. When using jars make sure they drain upside down.

Sprouting Containers

Jars

There are several types of containers that you can use. You can use one quart to half gallon glass jars, depending on the quantity of sprouts you will be using. Make sure these have the wide mouth openings in order for you to reach your hand down into the jar. There are special sprouting lids you can purchase, or you can use a nylon stretched over the top and held down with a rubber band.

Trays

There are several companies that make sprouting trays. Some of the trays are set up to stack upon each other and some have dividers so you can sprout several variety of seed at once.

Automatic sprout growers

Automatic sprout growers provide consistency they are rinsed often and because the are not handled as often the sprouts are more uniform.

Sprout Bags

Sprout bag are made of special nylon mesh screening. These were originally made for travel, but are becoming more popular for home use.

Sprouting Chart

Type of Seed	Amount For 1 Qt.	Soaking Time	Rinse (Cold) & Drain Daily
*Adzuki	1/4 cup	10-12 Hours	2-3 Times
Alfalfa	2 T.	4-6 Hours	3-4 Times
Almond	1/2 cup	10-12 Hours	2-3 Times
Amaranth	6 T.	8-10 minutes	3-4 Times
Barley	1/2 cup	4-8 Hours	3-4 Times
Beans	1/2 cup	12-24 Hours	3-4 Times
Beets	2 T.	6-8 Hours	3-4 Times
Cabbage	2 T.	4-8 Hours	2-3- Times
Clover	1 1/2 T.	4-8 Hours	2-4 Times
Corn	1/2 cup	8-12 Hours	2-3 Times
Cress	2 T.	8-10 minutes	3-4 Times
Fenugreek	1/4 cup	6-8 Hours	1-2 Times
Garbanzo	1/2 cup	8-12 Hours	3-4 Times
Green Pea	1/2 cup	8-12 Hours	3-4 Times
Lentil	1/2 cup	8-12 Hours	3-4 Times
Millet-unhulled	1/2 cup	6-8 Hours	3-4 Times
*Mung	1/4 cup	10-12 Hours	3-4 Times
Mustard	1/8 cup	8-10 minutes	*3-4 Times

Days to Harvest	Sprout Length at Harvest	Sprouting Hints
4-5 Days	1/2-1 inch	*Adzuki and Mung beans are sprouted different than other seeds.
4-6 Days	1-1 1/2 inches	Put in light 1-2 days before harvest
1 Day	0 inches	They do not sprout, they swell up
2-3 Days	1/4 inch	
3-4 Days	seed length	Steam lightly before eating
3-5 Days	1/4-1/2 inch	1 cup will fill a qt jar for canning sprouted beans** (Beans ch 4)
3-5 Days	1/4-1 inch	Longer sprouts - stronger flavor
3-5 Days	1/2-1 inch	Sprout in light last 2 days develops Chlorophyll when mature.
3-5 Days	1 - 1 1/2 inch	Sprout in light last 2 days develops Chlorophyll when mature.
2-3 Days	1/4-1/2 inch	Avoid over sprouting
3-5 Days	1/2 inch	Mist gently 3 times per day or mix with other seeds (spicy).
3-5 Days	1/2- 1 inch	Pungent flavor, mix with other seeds. Longer sprouts bitter taste.
2-3 Days	1/2 inch	Can mix with lentils & wheat
2-3 Days	1/4 - 1/2 inch	Split peas do not sprout use whole
2-5 Days	1/4 - 3/4 inch	Try both short and long sprouts
2-3 Days	1/4 inch	Use unhulled type.
3-6 Days	1/2-1 1/2 inch	Rinse for 1 minute with cold water
3-5 Days	1 inch	*Mist gently with cold water or mix with other seeds.

Sprouting Chart (Continued)

Type of Seed	Amount For 1 Qt.	Soaking Time	Rinse (Cold) & Drain Daily
Oats	1/2 cup	8-12 Hours	1-2 Times
Pumpkin	1 T.	8-12 Hours	1 Time
Radish	2 T.	4-8 Hours	3-4 Times
Rye	1/2 cup	8-12 Hours	3-4 Times
Sesame	1/4 - 1/2 cup	4-8 Hours	3-4 Times
Soybean	1/2 cup	*24 Hours	5-6 Times
*Sunflower	1/2 cup	6-8 Hours	3-4 Times
Triticale	1/2 cup	8-12 Hours	3-4 Times
Wheat	1/2 cup	8-12 Hours	3-4 Times

Mung & Adzuki Beans

Mung beans and Adzuki beans need to be grown under pressure. If not the sprouts will be thin, spindly and twisted. We want fat, straight, juicy sprouts.

Days to Harvest	Sprout Length at Harvest	Sprouting Hints
2-3 Days	1/4-1/2 inch	Whole oats Before eating remove remaining husks
1 Day	0 inches	Do not sprout, Swells up 1st day
3-6 Days	1/8-1 1/2 inch	Gets hotter as sprout grows, mix with other seeds, Sprout in light last 2 days develops chlorophyll.
2-3 Days	1/4-1/2 inch	Can mix with wheat & lentils,.eat with in 3 days. Only use whole unhulled berries.
1-2 Days	seed length	Will turn bitter if sprout is too long. Very small sprout.
3-6 Days	1/2 - 2 inches	Change soaking water every 8 hours. Ferments easily.
1-3 Days	0-1/2 inches	Sprouts are bitter after 2 inches long. Use hulled seeds. Can mix with alfalfa & grow 4-5 days.
1-3 Days	1/4 inch	Eat with in 3 days. Ferments very easy. Use same as wheat.
1-3 Days	1/4 inch	Can mix with other seeds for sweeter taste. Long or old sprouts get bitter.

A two pound cottage cheese or yogurt plastic container is perfect to grow these beans. From the inside poke holes through the bottom to let the water drain out. You will need to make a weight for the sprouts to push against. You can use an old nylon, cheese cloth, or sheet material. Make a bag the same size as the top of the container. Fill the bag with sterilized rocks or marbles.

Place 1/4 cup of bean seeds in the container. Cover the beans with the weighted bag. Set this container into a larger container and cover well with hot tap water and soak for 10 to 12 hours. Drain well, rinse at least three times a day by running water through the bag and out the bottom of the container for at least one minute each time you rinse.

It takes almost a week to get the sprouts full size the way we like them. By this time the container will be packed all the way full, with the bag setting on top of the container.

Remove the bag and put the sprouts in a large bowl with cool water. With your fingers swish back and forth to separate the beans from each other and to loose the shell. Some shells will float and others will fall to the bottom.

Drain the sprouts well and refrigerate in an air tight container. Place a folded paper towel in the bottom to absorb the extra water. They are now ready to eat. You can now add them to salads, stir fry, casseroles, sandwiches, soups, or just munch them. It cost about 4 to 6 cents for all those sprouts.

Sunflower Plants

Go beyond sunflower sprouts. Take a hand full of the soaked sunflower seeds and spread a layer over the top of the soil in a flower pot. Wad up paper towel and completely cover the seeds. Keep wet, warm and dark for 2 to 3 days. Remove the towels. The roots will go down into the soil and the plant will begin to grow. The plant will grow the first two leaves. When the plants are 2 to 4 inches tall or more they are ready to eat. Pinch off the stem as low as you can with out disturbing the other roots. Scissors make it easy to snip off one plant at a time. It taste like water crest with out being nippy.

Delsa Wilson's favorite sandwich in the whole world is one slice of whole wheat bread spread with avocado, filled with these sunflower plants and other sprouts. Fold it together and feast.

I want to thank her for her information on sprouting Mung and Adzuki Beans.

Juicing

Beyond Sprouting with Wheat and Barley

Growing your own Wheatgrass and Barleygrass is a super source of chlorophyll and it has a wide range of vitamins and minerals. Research has found that Wheatgrass juice is very similar to the molecular structure of hemin, which is part of our hemoglobin, the vital part of the blood which carries the oxygen throughout the body. The chlorophyll is a cell stimulator, rejuvenator, and red blood cell builder. It also helps purify the blood, which helps to cleanse the kidneys, liver, and urinary tract.

Juice from the wheat and barley grasses are very potent and full of antioxidants. In juice form your body can assimilate the nutrients quickly and efficiently. They work as natural healers to the body.

When consuming Wheatgrass juice, start out slowly 1oz per day working up to 4-6oz per day is usually sufficient. You can then follow your drink with a glass of distilled water. If you are working on a health crisis you may want to increase your consumption of Wheatgrass juice and consider Wheatgrass juice implants. Make sure you are drinking plenty of distilled water as this juice is working to clean and rebuild your system.

Wheatgrass juice is used at many famous cancer clinics throughout the world and has had miraculous results.

When growing the Wheat, Barley, Rye, or Spelt for grass, you need soil and at least three flats the same size, one you will use for a lid. For each flat you would soak 1 to 1 1/2 cups of hard red wheat or barley for 12 hours or overnight. Then rinse and drain the wheatberries about every three to four hours for the next 12 hours to prevent the berries from drying out. When the wheat has sprouted with approximately 1/4 inch tails they are ready to put on top of the soil mixture. You make a mixture or buy a mixture of 50% topsoil and 50% peat moss. In your flat you would fill the soil mixture to a depth of 1-1/2 inches. You will then thoroughly moisten the soil by sprinkling or spraying with water. Do not soak the soil. Then spread the berries evenly on top of the soil. Be careful not to break the sprouts. Next place one of the containers on top for the first three days. This will keep the moisture in and the light out. On the forth day you will remove the cover, water the sprouting grass and set the container in sunlight. Make sure your flats are able to drain. There is a learning curve to growing wheatgrass, the trick is not to let the seeds dry out, as they are just setting on top of the soil, let them get plenty of air circulating, and make sure the dirt is moist and well drained. This works best if you have the flats on a slant. The common problem with wheat grass is mold. The grass will be ready to cut and juice on the seventh day. The grass should be 6 to 8 inches high. Each flat should yield about 8 to 16 ounces of juice, depending on how thick your grass is.

When growing your wheatgrass you should learn about composting. It is as simple as getting a plastic garbage can. Then drill or poke holes all around and at the bottom for air circulation, and drainage if your soil happens to be too wet.

You would break up the flat of soil after your grass has been cut and juiced, and make this the bottom layer. This soil will be totally full of roots. Next take two heaping hands filled with earthworms and place them on top of the broken flat of soil.

Then layer with vegetable scraps and used wheatgrass soil. Do not use any fruit scraps, this will bring unwanted pests and an unpleasant aroma. That's all you need to do, the earth worms will do the rest.

As you continue to grow your grasses to juice, you will want to expand to a second trash container. Using the first one for soil to put in your new flats while the second container of soil, vegetable scraps, and earthworms are in the process of composting.

In this way you make sure you put back to the soil all the nutrients that were used. The plants can not pull out nutrients from the soil that are not there.

I would also suggest purchasing a Wheatgrass juicer. Most juicers will not juice the grasses properly. However if you can't purchase a juicer right away and you want to start getting the benefits of the wheatgrass juice you can put the cut grass in a blender, add distilled water liquefy, and drink. If you choose to do it this way to begin with, you will soon see the need for a wheatgrass juicer.

Storing

What to store first
The choice is yours

There are several ways to start your food storage process and we will discuss some of them. What I would like to do is group several categories. The first group will be the life-sustaining group. This may look overwhelming, however the first group will be the easiest and the fastest group to obtain. I have a list of a variety of grains and beans. You do not have to store every one of these. Pick out your favorites and then add a few grains that are new to you and your family. This will add variety to your meals. You can adjust to your family's preference and needs.

DON'T MAKE THIS OVERWHELMING

Remember the amounts of grains, beans, sweeteners, and other foods that are listed are the amounts needed if you had no other foods to live on. Groups 1, 2, and 3 will last for many years. I originally removed Group 4 because it is the least healthy group, but because of the request of my friend I have put this group back in this book. Group 4 must be rotated within one year to prevent spoilage, even though some can goods will last up to five years. Early rotation will be the key to the best nutrients available in a canned product.

Learn to use the foods in Group 1 and 2. If you will make these foods part of your meals every day, your health will greatly improve. If you have children you will see a change in their behavior, their minds will become more alert and clear, and they will be more satisfied and content. They will be able to concentrate better in school. You will be eliminating much of the preservatives, artificial flavors and colorings, unnecessary fats, and all the additives put into our foods. You will also notice you will be spending less on your food bill each month.

Our food is best fresh, then dehydrated if dried at a low temperature, then frozen, and lastly canned. Any time you can incorporate fresh fruits and vegetables in your diet the better, that is why you should learn to sprout and juice your sprouts and grasses. Your sprouts and grasses won't have the sprays or contaminants that most commercial vegetables have.

If you will incorporate Juicing into you diet you will find a burst of energy that the vitamins, minerals, enzymes, and amino acids will supply to your depleting body. Juicing is time consuming in the preparation of the fruits and vegetables, but worth every minute.

For example to sustain life for one person you would need approximately 400lbs of grains, a combination of 350lbs of wheat and 75lbs of other grains or 300lbs of wheat and 175lbs of other grains. Store the greater portion of grain as wheat. It can be a combination of the alkaline wheats and the regular wheats. Remember once the wheat is sprouted it activates enzymes that makes wheat easy to digest.

Start out to purchase a one year supply of grains and beans for one person. When you purchase this amount and if you have 2 people in your household you now have a 6 months supply of grains. If you have 4 people you now have a 3 months supply of grains and beans if that is all you had to live on. Don't think you have to go out and purchase everything at once. Be consistent, make a purchasing plan and stick to it.

Group 1

This is the basic group which should be purchased first for survival and health.

Grains, Beans and Lentils, Sweeteners, Oils, Powder Milk (or extra soybeans to be made into milk they store longer and are better for you), Salt, and Vitamin C

Grains (400 lbs. per person mostly Wheat, Spelt, or Kamut along with a good mixture of other grains).

Wheat, hard	Wheat, soft	Millet
Barley	Corn	Rye
Oats	Quinoa	Buckwheat
Amaranth	Spelt	Kamut
Triticale	etc.	

Beans, Rice, and other Legumes (60 lbs. per person).

Adzuki	Black beans	Blackeye peas
Garbanzo	Great Northern	Kidney beans
Soybeans	Mung beans	Split Peas
Alaska Peas	Lima beans	Pinto beans
Navy beans	English Peas	Brown rice
White rice	Flaxseed	Green Lentils
Red Lentils	etc.	

Sweeteners (60 lbs. per person).

Honey	Molasses	Stevia powder
Sorghum	Barley syrup	Brown rice syrup
Sucanat	Turbinado sugar	Maple syrup
Fructose	Dried fruit	Brown sugar
Jams & Jellies	Corn syrup	Fruit drink powder
Unsweetened coconut		

Powdered Milk or Soy Beans (16 lbs. per person).
Or you can add additional soybeans, sweet brown rice, or nuts if you are going to make your own fresh milks. Again I would suggest a soy milk machine for ease and convenience, it only takes twelve minutes to make nutritious milks.

Fats and Oil (2 to 6 gallons per person).
Olive oil – cold pressed extra virgin (organic if you can afford it) or a combination of any of the good oils. Purchase your oil in the size of container that you would consume in one month. This will help so your oil does not go rancid by being exposed to air and light. Most oils when opened should be refrigerated the exception is olive oil and it should be kept in a dark place. Olive oil and Canola oil should be used for cooking, most of the other oils should not be heated.

Vitamin C (500mg /day minimum per person) or a good natural food supplement that contains vitamin C along with other vitamins, minerals, and amino acids not synthetic. The 500mg per day is the bare minimum of vitamin C, you may increase to 1000mg per day along with Vit. E.

Salt (8 to 10 lbs. per person) Sea Salt, Celtic Salt, or Real Salt preferred.

Group 2

Baking powder – Aluminum Free (6 lbs. per person).

Baking Soda (8 lbs. per person).

Vinegar (1 to 2 gallons per person).

Sprouting Seeds (10 lbs. per person minimum)

Alfalfa	Almonds	Amaranth
Anise	Barley unhulled	Beans
Beans Adzuki	Beans Black-Eye	Beans Kidney
Beans Mung	Beans Pinto	Broccoli
Buckwheat	Cabbage	Canola
Clover-Red	Corn	Fenugreek
Flax seed	Garbanzo	Lentils Green
Lentils Red	Lettuce	Millet
Mustard Seed	Oats unhulled	Peas
Pumpkin seeds	Quinoa	Radish seeds
Rice Brown	Rye	Sesame
Soybeans	Spinach	Triticale
Vegetable seeds	Watercress	Wheat

Seasonings and Spices

Herbs or spices that are particularly healing include cayenne, curry, ginger, and garlic.

Although spices are consumed in small amounts, they are concentrated and therefore nutrient dense, contributing vitamin A, carotene, vitamin B-6, calcium, iron, magnesium, and zinc to the food supply (*Center for Nutrition Policy and Promotion/USDA*).

Allspice	Almond ext.	Anise seed	Arrowroot
Basil	Bay leaves	Bullion Beef	Bullion Ckn.
Bullion vegan	Caraway seed	Cardamom	Carob powder
Cayenne	Celery seed	Chili powder	Cinnamon
Cloves powder	Cloves whole	Coriander	Thyme
Cumin	Curry	Dill seed	Dry Mustard
Fennel Seed	Fenugreek	Garlic	Ginger
Vanilla extract	Kelp	Lemon	Sumac
Lemon juice	Mace	Maple extract	Marjoram
Mint	Miso	Mustard seed	Nutmeg
Onion Flakes	Onion powder	Oregano	Parsley
Paprika	Pepper	Poppy seeds	Rosemary
Saffron	Sage	Savory	Seasoned Salts
Sesame seeds	Soy Sauce	Spearmint	Tarragon
Vanilla extract	Turmeric	Vanilla bean	
Cream of Tarter		Worcestershire sauce	
Italian Seasoning		Any other Favorite Spices	

Un-flavored gelatin (3 to 4 - 8oz. Box per person) or Augar-augar (is a seaweed combination, it has no taste and no fishy smell).

Agar is a sea algae, and is healthier than gelatin which is made from animal by-products. It is a fibrous thickener used to thicken many desserts.

Group 3

Dry Soup Mix (2 - #10 cans per person)

Dairy

Butter, dehydrated (1 to 2 - #10 cans per person) will store 2-3 years.

Butter milk solids, dehydrated (1 - #10 can per person) will store 2-3 years.

Cheese, dehydrated powder (1 to 2 - #10 cans per person) will store 3-5 years.

Eggs, dehydrated (2 - #10 cans per person).

Egg whites dehydrated (2 - #10 cans per person).

Vegetables Dehydrated   (2 - #10 cans per person)
will store up to 8 years.

Vegetables Freeze dried will last up to fifteen years.

Potatoes	Carrots	String Beans	Peas
Onions	Garlic	Celery	
Tomato Powdered			
Any other Dehydrated Vegetables			

Fruits Dehydrated – No Sulfur added (3 - #10 cans per person) will store up to 8 years.

Fruits Freeze dried will last up to fifteen years.

Apples	Peaches	Pears	Apricots
Raisins	Bananas	Lemon juice or powder	
Any other Dehydrated Fruits			

Group 4.

Remember canned items are the least nutritional and are mainly for convenience and familiarity to your family.

Group 4 has the shortest shelf life and should be consumed within one year. Some can goods will last up to five years with proper temperature control, but as the years go by the nutrients will diminish.

If the acid content of the fruit or vegetables are high you may want to rotate them within a six to nine month period to prevent spoilage.

The suggested amounts are based on a 52-week plan. Example: if you would eat two cans of meat per week you would store 104 cans of meat. The same thing with canned fruits, if you would consume one can a week you would buy 52 cans of fruit.

You need to personalize your food storage for your family. Store what your family likes and what you will use. Remember get only enough for one year. As you use one can replace it with another.

I would first recommend buying like this for only one person, even if you have four or more people in your family. You can then gage what your family's needs are within a few months and then buy accordingly.

Don't buy more can goods than you can use in a year. You don't want to buy food and have it go bad before you can consume it. Waste is not part of an ideal food storage plan.

This group of food is for convenience, added variety, and familiarity for your family, not necessarily for nutrition. The fruits and vegetables can be used for an additional source of liquid in a time of need.

Canned Meats (1 can per person per week). This will also depend if you have frozen meats. There are a variety of meats that you can choose from:

Bass	Bluefish	Butterfish	Bream
Grouper	Haddock	Halibut	Kipper
Salmon	Sardine	Red Snapper	Soul
Trout	Whiting		

Chicken	Cornish Hen	Ground Beef	Roast Beef
Lamb	Mutton	Turkey	Veal

Canned Fruits (2 cans per person per week).
There are a variety of fruits that you can choose from:

Apples	Apricots	Cherries	Peaches
Pears	Any other favorite fruits		

Canned Vegetables (2 cans per person per week).
The choice is up to you.

Canned Soup (1 can per person per week).

Canned Stew (2 cans per person per month).

Macaroni, Noodles, Spaghetti, etc. (1 pound per person per month).

Tapioca (1 pound per person per year).

Creating Your
One
Year Supply

Creating your year supply

When I suggest different ways to purchase your food storage you can use any combination of the following, or create your own method. These are just suggestions to get you started and to give you a visual perception of the amount of storage you will need.

First purchase your long-term basic survival food storage. Wheat, Grains, Powder Milk, Honey, Oil, Vitamin C, Baking Powder, Baking Soda, and Salt.

Purchase by the pound

You can do this by setting a budget and sticking with it. You set the number of pounds of grain you will buy each week or each month. This can be 25lbs per week, or 25lbs per person per week. Or 25lbs per month, or 25lbs per person per month. What ever you set to purchase, you will find great satisfaction when this is accomplished. If you only get a month's supply of food for your family, it means your family is taken care for a month no matter what crisis may come upon you. And you know the quality of food you have purchased.

Purchase by budgeting your money

You can also use the $5 or $10 dollar a week method. That is you set aside five or ten dollars a week and purchase your food storage. Some weeks you may not be able to purchase what you want for $10. You would put this money aside each week and in the following weeks you would purchase what you need. Little by little you will have your basic food storage complete and be able to continue to build on your every day necessities.

Purchase by the bucket

One 5 gallon bucket holds approximately 35 pounds of wheat or grain. For one adult person you would need about 9 buckets. This would be approximately four hundred and twenty pounds of grain.

Purchase by the can

One #10 can holds approximately 5 pounds of wheat or grain. For one adult person you would need to store about 80 #10 cans. If you have the boxes that hold 6 of these #10 cans, this would equal 13 cases plus 2 cans. This would be approximately four hundred pounds of grains, depending on how tight you packed each can.

If you will purchase the recommended amounts of foods in group-one, your basic survival group you know you can sustain your family's life for one year. If you use these foods to supplement your daily needs the cost of your weekly food bill will go down and the health of your family will increase.

Although this is set up for a year supply, and these foods will last longer than a year if stored properly. This food is not meant to sit on your shelf. They are meant for your use, to maintain good health and to be more self-reliant.

Equipment

Equipment Needed

This list of equipment, some you will absolutely need and others will be most helpful in your endeavors to live a more healthy life from the foods you have stored.

- Hand Mill
- Electric Mill
- Water Purifiers....Plain bleach 5.25% Sodium Hypochlorite....Water Distiller....Containers to hold emergency water (14 gallons per person) more if you have room (It takes approx. 2 ½ gallons of water to flush a toilet)
- Seed Sprouter or glass jars with nylon or netting
- Dehydrator (low temperature under 120 degrees).
- Electric Mixer
- Blender
- Bread Mixer (this is not the same as a bread machine)
- Juicer.... The Champion Juicer is an excellent juicer for the price, you can add the wheat grass in with other vegetables and get some of the juice extracted (although this is not the most effective way to juice wheat grass). The Green Power Juice Extractor...this juicer is made to do Wheatgrass as well as other vegetables. You can also get a grinder attachment for your grains with either juicer.
- Wheat grass juicer does juice grasses and some soft fruits only. You can purchase a hand juicer or an electric juicer. The hand crank juicer is hard to use and not as convenient as the electric juicer.

- Mini grain grinder (they are commonly known as coffee grinders) a must have for Flax seed, and other dry Herbs. You can also grin a few teaspoons of grain at a time for baby cereal.
- Meat grinder, if you are living off the land.
- Crockpot
- Soy Milk Maker - used for making soy milk, almond milk, rice milk, tofu, and nut butters.

How
&
Where to Store Food

Everyone has room to store the Essentials! The Choice Is Yours

Lets talk about ways to store food and other storage items. The ideal situation would be to have a cool dark room in a dry basement set up for just food storage. It would be one very large pantry or your very own little food store. It would have a temperature ranging no more than 70 degrees and no less than 50 degrees. You would also want to store very top quality food items.

With the rising cost of food and the uncertain times we live in, food storage is a wise investment for all of us both monetarily and mentally. When a disaster strikes, the time to prepare is gone. When you are prepared, you can turn your thoughts and emotions to your loved ones.

In your storage, you will probably have a combination of all three of these containers: cans, glass, and plastic. There are advantages and disadvantages to all.

There are good and bad points to every type of storage container. You need to decide which ones are best for you, your family and your environment. Metal containers; can rust. You never want to set cans directly on a cement floor; they will absorb the moisture from the cement. Your glass containers; can break. Make sure they are in a secure place. You can store in plastic buckets, but they can burn in a fire. The Foil Pouches need to be stored in a protected area away from rodents that can eat through the bags.

Your intention is to store your food in a way that you block out moisture from getting in the container, and that it will not attract bugs or rodents. You also want to make sure rodents cannot eat through the container. An airtight container will eliminate most problems. Make sure your storage area is kept clean at all times.

When filling your container it is important to pack the food as tight as you can. To compact the food you would pick up the container slightly from the surface and tap it several times on the table, or on the floor if you are filling your five-gallon containers. This is eliminating excess air from the container and allows you to store more food in fewer containers. Again we want an undesirable atmosphere for pest to exist.

Bulk items such as Wheat, Beans, Salt, Pasta, etc. can be stored in five-gallon food grade buckets. These can be purchased from companies that sell Plastics, Industrial, and Laboratory Supplies. You might want to ask your local Fast Food place for their used buckets. Make sure the lid is not damaged, if it is, all you need to purchase is a new lid. You will need to clean the containers. After cleaning the containers your final rinse can be hydrogen peroxide mixed with water to sanitize the container or you can sanitize the container with a bleach solution. Fill the five gallon bucket half full of water, add 1/4 cup 5.25% or 6% sodium hypochlorite house hold bleach. Then continue to fill the bucket to the top.with water. Drain the solution from the bucket and rinse thoroughly. Make sure the buckets are completely dry before using them for any food storage.

Dry Ice method

I personally don't use this method, you can burn the grains if not done properly, it is inconvenient and in some places the dry ice is expensive and hard to find. Although this process is fine for killing bugs in your grains.

When storing in your five-gallon bucket, you may add dry ice to your whole grains, beans, rice, pasta, or dried fruit and vegetables. The dry ice helps remove the oxygen from the bucket. The dry ice can either be placed on the bottom of the bucket or in the middle. Make sure you wipe off any excess moisture from the dry ice before putting it in the bucket and place a protective barrier between the ice and the grains to eliminate the possibility of freezer burn. You would use about 2oz of dry ice per five-gallon bucket. Just place the lid on the bucket, but do not seal until all the ice has evaporated. If the bucket is sealed before the ice has evaporated the bucket could expand and burst.

Oxygen absorber packets

The oxygen absorber packets can be used with whole grains, rice, beans, pasta, flour, etc. Do not use with any product containing egg, and do not add oxygen absorbers in with sugar, it will get very hard. It does not however ruin the sugar. The purpose of these packets is to remove any oxygen still in the bucket or container and to make an environment where insects cannot live.

Bay Leaves

I personally have never had an infestation in any of my storage items. I store and use as many organic items as possible. One advantage of organic grains is that the soil is cultivated in such a way that nutrients are added back, therefore raising the nutrition level in the plants and thus allowing the healthy plant to fight off infestations naturally with very little chemicals to weaken the plant. I have always stored my food in the old fashion way using bay leaves. I put four or five bay leaves at the bottom of my five-gallon bucket, then four or five in the middle, then another four or five bay leaves at the top. I compress my grains and beans as tight as I can and fill the bucket as close to the top as I can, and steel get the lid closed. In order to close the lid I have to stand with my heels on the rim of the bucket lid (make sure you have something you can hold on to) and slightly putting my weight up and down as I go around the rim of the bucket.

I still use bay leaves when I store my food. I have never used the dry ice method. I use the oxygen absorber packets when storing commercial pastas (make sure they do not contain egg) or other non-living food items. Whole grains can be stored at least twenty to thirty years if stored properly. The moisture content must be less than 10%. I have gotten Hard Red Winter Wheat with only 3% moisture. Moisture content will very with different grains.

I have read that bay leaves do not keep infestations from happening. I don't know the reason why I have never had a problem. It maybe that I keep my storage area clean and free from spillage that would attract bugs. I keep a tight lid on all my containers. I buy clean organic grains with a low moisture content, or the combination of all the above, but for the added peace of mind I will continue to use bay leaves in my grains, beans, and lentils.

Diatomaceous Earth

Horticultural grade diatomaceous earth (as opposed to the cheaper, less effective product used in swimming pool filters) is a non-toxic, safe substance made up from crushed fossils of freshwater organisms and marine life. Crushed to a fine powder and observed through a microscope, the particles resemble bits of broken glass.

Diatomaceous earth is the remains of microscopic one-celled plants (phytoplankton) called diatoms that lived in the oceans that once covered the western part of the United States and other parts of the world. Huge deposits were left behind when the water receded. They are now mined and have several important uses. Natural DE also makes a very effective natural insecticide. The insecticide quality of DE is due to the razor sharp edges of the diatom remains. When DE comes contact with the insects, the sharp edges lacerate the bugs' waxy exoskeleton and then the powdery DE absorbs the body fluids causing death from dehydration. Said more simply, DE kills insects by drying then up. You'll see how drying DE is if you handle it with bare hands.

There is no residual danger of contamination. However, there are a few precautions. Diatomaceous earth is very dusty and can cause lung problems if breathed heavily, so when applying it dry always wear a good dust mask. The second precaution is that DE sold for swimming pool filters is ineffective for insect control because it has been heated and chemically treated. It won't kill insects and it is very dangerous to breathe.

Use 5% by weight in stored grains. Diatomaceous Earth: The "Silver Bullet" by Howard Garrett.

Where do I put all this food?

Where do you put your buckets? This is where you become creative. The ideas listed here are going to be for those that do not have their own area for their own little food store. Now remember the cooler the better. The ideal temperature would be 68 degrees.

You can make a night stand two buckets high, place a round top on it and a cloth.

You can place the buckets under a bed put the box springs and mattress on top. If the buckets seem too tall under your bed, you can raise the bed with either cement or wood blocks to the height that you want and then use that space for other storage.

You can make shelves with them for a closet. You can put a bucket at either end of a closet. You can place a board on top, and put shoes, or other items on the floor between the buckets and on top of the board adding more storage area.

If you have a little extra space on the side of your washer, you can use double stick tape to adhere a piece of insulation board to the side of the washer facing your storage buckets. This will keep the heat from the hot water to be in direct contact with the buckets. In most cases you can store two deep and at least three high. Make sure your containers are sealed tight to eliminate moisture from getting in.

Another space that can be utilized is under your TV. You can stack two deep, two high, and either two or three wide.

Cover this with a thin piece of plywood put a tablecloth or other skirting to match, or accent your décor. You can use this same principle for a computer desk, sewing machine stand, or a study desk for the children. The only difference would be to eliminate the middle buckets for leg room. You can also angle this in a corner and use the concealed space for additional storage.

If you have a back door entrance where you take off your shoes you can possibly stack two deep and two high on the back row this will add to your storage space and allow the shoes to be stacked neatly.

If you have a small laundry area there is usually a shelf above the washer and dryer. There is normally room to add an extra shelf above. This shelf could be used to store extra storage items such as laundry soap, cleaning supplies, etc. You just need to make sure if you store powdered laundry detergent that you place a bag around it to keep the moisture from making the soap hard. Again this does not hurt the soap, but can make it very hard to where you would have to break it up before you could use it.

Organizing your cabinet shelves is essential to your over-all storage. Eliminate the clutter. You can have a year supply of tooth past in a very small area. You can add extra side and or rear shelves to your bathroom cabinets to store smaller items. Make every usable space count.

Remember be creative. You do, and can make room for the "Essentials of Life" food storage. You just have to do it. Consider the size and shapes of your containers to fit your creative storage spaces.

Storing Can Goods

According to Food Marketing Institute – For Consumers
www.fmi.org/consumer/foodkeeper/pantry.htm

Shelf stable foods such as canned goods, cereal, baking mixes, pasta, dry beans, mustard, etc. can be kept safely at room temperature. To keep these foods at their best quality, store in clean, dry, and in cool (below 85 degrees F) cabinets away from the stove or the refrigerator's exhaust.

Extremely hot (over 100 degrees F) and cold temperatures are harmful to canned goods. At temperatures above 100 degrees F, thermo-philic spores will germinate. This microbial growth can cause reduced shelf life and reduced quality of the food.

Never use food from cans that are leaking, bulging, badly dented, or with a foul order, cracked jars or jars with loose or bulging lids; or any container that spurts liquid when you open it. Never taste such foods. Throw out any food you suspect is spoiled.

In general, most canned foods have a long "health life," and when properly stored, are safe to eat for several years: Low-acid canned goods – 2 to 3 years (canned meat and poultry, stews, pasta products, potatoes, corn, carrots, spinach, beans, beets, peas, pumpkin and soups except tomato).

High acid canned goods – 12 to 18 months (tomato products, fruits, sauerkraut and foods in vinegar-based sauces or dressings).

Inventory Chart

Basic Food Storage Inventory

Enter the amounted needed for your family per year. This chart can be used any way you want: 1 can, 1 bucket, 1 case, 1 week, 1 month, etc.

PRODUCT	1	2	3	4	5	6	7	8	9
Water									
Wheat									
Legumes									
Oils									
Honey									
Dry Milk									
Baking Soda									
Salt									

10	11	12	13	14	15	16	17	18	19	20	21	22

72-Hour
Disaster Emergency Kit

72-Hour Disaster Emergency Kit

The best time to prepare is before a disaster. Your family will cope best if they are familiar with the plan you have set up and the foods you have packed for them. The best carry container for your kit is a backpack. Have these where you can access them easily.

Water is essential, it is the most important item in your kit, but it is also heavy to carry. Find ways to strap canteens, water bottles, or soda bottles filled with water to the out side of your backpack. You may also want to add water purification supplies, such as iodine tablets, 2 percent tincture of iodine, Halazone tablets, and or liquid bleach (do not use scented bleaches only use bleach that contains 5% sodium hypochlorite, a chlorine compound as it's only active ingredient). Add 2 drops of bleach for each quart of clear water, four drops per quart if the water is cloudy. Let the water stand 30 minutes. If you do not smell or taste the chlorine add another dose of bleach wait another 15 minutes and then test again. You may want to include small siphon hose and cotton balls (for filtering material from the siphoned water). Note Iodine is toxic and may cause allergic reactions in some people. Neither bleach, Iodine, nor Halazone tablets are 100% effective against all water borne pathogens.

Store one gallon of water per day for each person (two quarts for drinking, two quarts for food preparation and sanitation). Children and nursing mother will need more water. If water has been treated with iodine tablets or bleach, it might not be as pleasant to drink. You may want to add powdered drink mixes to your kit to make the drinking water more pleasant.

Learn all you can about water, how to dig a well, how to purify water and how to catch dew and rain water.

Your 72-Hour kit can be as simple as providing a three day supply of food and water or it can expand to include: First aid kit, Clothing, Bedding, Shelter, and Cooking items. Here is an example of my 72-hour **Survival** food kit. You can very this to your needs and liking. Remember you should pack high caloric and nutritious food.

Day 1	**Day 2**	**Day 3**
Breakfast	**Breakfast**	**Breakfast**
½ cup cracked wheat	½ cup cracked wheat	½ cup cracked wheat
8 oz water (4oz to soak Wheat cereal)	8 oz water (4oz to soak wheat cereal)	8 oz water (4oz to soak wheat cereal)
1 or 2 packets of honey	1 or 2 packets of honey	1 or 2 packets of honey

1 multiple vitamin/mineral supplement each morning with breakfast.

Morning Snack	**Morning Snack**	**Morning Snack**
4 oz Raisins	4 oz Raisins	4oz Raisins
4 oz Water	4 oz Water	4 oz Water

Lunch	**Lunch**	**Lunch**
4 oz Trail Mix	4 oz Trail Mix	4 oz Trail Mix
1 Granola bar	1 Granola bar	1 Granola bar
8 oz Water	8 oz Water	8 oz Water

Afternoon Snack	**Afternoon Snack**	**Afternoon Snack**
1 oz Jerky	1 oz Jerky	1 oz Jerky
4-6 oz Water	4-6 oz Water	4-6 oz Water

Dinner	**Dinner**	**Dinner**
½ cup Soup Mix	½ cup Soup Mix	½ cup Soup Mix
8-12 oz Water (4 oz used for soup mix)	8-12 oz Water (4 oz used for soup mix)	8-12 oz Water (4 oz used for soup mix)

1 multiple vitamin/mineral supplement each evening with dinner.

Each Day	**Each Day**	**Each Day**
5 pieces of hard candy	5 pieces of hard candy	5 pieces of hard candy
1 pack of gum	1 pack of gum	1 pack of gum

I also throw in 3 small cans of spaghetti, ravioli, beans, etc. with pull off lids incase not enough water is left by evening to soak the grains or soups.

You will need 1 small container with an airtight lid to soak cracked wheat and soup (you could throw in some zip lock bags). At bedtime you would put your cracked wheat in the container with the 4oz of water (it takes approximately 4 hours for cracked wheat to get soft). After Breakfast or lunch put in the soup mix to soak until dinnertime.

I personally use a seal & serve to make sure everything is sealed airtight. Then I bag each day together for convince and to make sure the smaller children don't get confused.

You may also add hot cocoa mix, apple cider mix, tang (these are good to cover the taste of any water you may have to purify), canned fruit, canned juices, powdered milk, fruit roll ups, or other dried fruits, canned meats, high dosage B-Complex for stress, etc. This is your kit make it to suit your needs. Remember the more you add the longer the survival time the heavier the pack. Make sure the weight and content is compatible with the age and health of each person.

You will want to line your backpack with several garbage bags. These bags will keep everything dry, the additional bags can be used as a raincoat, and they can be used to catch rain and dew for additional drinking water, for lying on the ground to protect your self from moisture. You will find many uses for these bags.

When adding clothes to your kit you should include one change of clothing including an extra pair of shoes and two pairs of socks. Heavy-duty gloves and sun glasses. You might want to add a bandanna that can be tied around your nose and mouth as an air filter for pollen, etc., or used to help filter water, used as a bandage if necessary. You will find many uses for the bandanna.

You should also have some money put away with your emergency kits. Nothing higher than twenty dollar bills. Make sure you have plenty of small bills and change. The change can be stored in a hot water bottle. This will prevent the coins from breaking through any bags, sacks, etc. and the hot water bottle can be used for many other uses as well.

Food Storage is not Hoarding or a Fad it is a way of Life

The truth is, pure whole foods are the best thing for your body. That's whole grains, soybeans and other legumes, sprouting, fresh fruits and vegetables, juicing and distilled water.

You might think with all the abundant food around us, why would you need to store food? In knowing the seasons and how weather can effect crops and how pests can devour crops in such a short period time, natural disasters, and now more than ever the possible threat of food contamination makes you realize how vulnerable our food supply can be.

We are and have been living in the land of plenty. We help feed the world, but as a society we do not take advantage of what we have. Even now if we hear of an upcoming storm the Grocery Store shelves are stripped clean of bread and milk and other supplies within hours. If you are prepared you shall not fear the perils of the world. You can sit back in your home and know you can take care of your family and loved ones.

Food storage is not just for times of disasters of nature. There are thousands of people loosing their jobs. What comfort, food storage gives at times like this. Another excellent reason to store whole grains and to use them is for nutrition. Processed foods do not have the same nutrients and fiber that is greatly needed in this fast food world we now live in. A lot of our illnesses are caused by years of poor eating habits.

By the time the wheat and other grains are milled and processed the nutrients have been destroyed and the fiber has been removed. At that point the manufactures enrich our food with synthetic vitamins and minerals then turn around and sell us the fiber in powder or pills. As a society intestinal problems are on the increase. By eating whole grains, beans, and rice in your daily diet you can greatly reduce the risk of intestinal problems and other health related diseases.

Food storage saves you money. Whole grains, beans, rice and lentils cost less than processed foods, are more nourishing, and they are more satisfying than processed foods. I can't imagine running to the store every time I want to prepare a meal, for lack of the ingredients needed. How convenient it is to just go to your own pantry and get what you need.

Remember Store nutritious foods and learn to eat what you store. Rotation along with variety is the key. If you have never stored whole grains, learn a few great recipes and introduce them to your family before it becomes a necessity. Learn to sprout and to juice and grow wheat and barley grass. You can make this a great learning adventure while adding health, self reliance, and stability to your life.

Recipes

COOKING TIMES FOR GRAINS

Grains 1 cup dry	Water (cups)	Cooking time	Yield (cups)
Amaranth	1½ - 2½	20-25 min.	2
Barley (whole)	3	1 hr 15 min.	3 ½
Basmati (brown	2	45 min.	3
Basmati (white)	1 ¾	15-20 min.	2 ½
Brown rice	2	1 hr	3
Buckwheat (kasha)	2	15 min.	2 ½
Bulgur wheat	2	15-20 min.	3
Coarse cornmeal (polenta)	4	25 min.	3
Couscous (pre-cooked)	2	5 min.	2 ½
Cracked wheat	2	25 min.	2 ¼
Kamut	2 ½ -3	1 ½ -2 hrs.	2
Millet	2	30 min.	4
Rolled oats	1 ½	10 min.	2
Spelt	1 ½	30-40 min.	2
Teff	4	15-20 min.	2
Wild rice	2 ½	50-60 min.	4
Whole wheat	3	2 hrs.	2 ½
Quinoa	2	15 min.	3
Brown rice	2	1 hr.	3

COOKING TIMES FOR BEANS AFTER SOAKING 24 HOURS

Beans 1 cup dry	Water (cups)	Cooking time	Yield (cups)
Adzuki	3	1 hr.	2
Anasaz	4	1 hr.	2 ½
Black beans	4	1 ½ hrs.	2
Black-eyed peas	3	1 hr.	2
Garbanzo (chick peas)	4	3 hrs.	2
Great Northern	3 ½	2 hrs.	2
Kidney beans	3	1 ½ hrs.	2
Lentils & Split peas	3	45 min.	2 ¼
Limas	3	1 ½ hrs.	1 ¼
Baby limas	2	1 ½ hrs	1 ¾
Mung	3	45 min.	2
Pinto beans	3	2 ½ hrs.	2
Red beans	3	1-1 ½ hrs.	2
Small white beans (navy)	3	2 hrs.	2
Soybeans	4	3 hrs. or more	2
Soy grits	2	15 min.	2

BULGUR WHEAT

BULGUR WHEAT: Wheat, is either soaked or cooked until the outer layer of the wheat begins to split, then dried and ground.

TO PREPARE: Fill a large pan ½ full of wheat. Cover the wheat with water (about 1 in. above the wheat). Bring to a boil stirring often to keep from burning. Boil until water is gone. You can spread the wheat directly on the table if it is water resistant (glass, etc.), or you can lay plastic table cloth over your table. Spread the wheat out onto the cloth and spread the wheat as thin as you can. The thinner the wheat is spread the faster it will dry. This will take approximately 1-2 days (you must use a fan) to dry. Make sure that you rake the wheat with your fingers at least 4 times a day until wheat is completely dry. This should then be stored in a cool dry place. It is now ready to crack or grind depending on your recipe.

SOUP KUFTA WITH YOGURT

Wheat Mixture:
4 cups - Wheat (use fine ground bulgur wheat).
2-1/2 to 3 lbs. - Cube steak meat (this is ground about 5 times and has no fat on it).
2 Large or 3 medium onions (finely diced).
1/2 tsp. Cayenne pepper
Salt to taste (about 3 Tbs. Or more).

Filling:
mix together
1 lb. Butter softened
1 lb. Chopped walnuts

Broth:
Take 1 large soup bone with some meat if possible (this is a real treat if you find a piece of meat in your soup bowl), then place it in a pan with approximately two gallons of distilled water. Simmer all day. Add salt and pepper to taste.

Gradually add water to the wheat mixture and mix well. *Don't get the mixture soggy.* It's very important that your wheat mixture is kneaded very well. Mixture should be like medium soft dough. Dip hands in cold water and make balls the size of a golf ball. Then, make a dent in the middle with your thumb and press all around the inside wall to make a round opening for the filing. The thinner the wall the more successful your kufta will be. Place the filling in this hole and bring open edges of the kufta together sealing and smoothing the surface with wet fingers. Cook in prepared broth about five minutes. Then add

1-1/2 quarts yogurt and 1 Tbs. of dried mint. Cook an additional 5-8 minutes. *Be careful when removing the kufta so as not to puncture or break the balls.* Serve immediately.

PAN KUFTA

Filling:
Sauté
1 lb. extra lean ground beef
4 Large onions (finely diced)
Add salt and pepper to taste
Drain off any fat and add ½ lb. chopped walnuts

Use the same wheat mixture as (Soup Kufta with Yogurt) except substitute cube steak with very lean ground beef. Spread mixture in greased pan about ½ full. Add filling and add another layer of wheat mixture. Cut diagonally about 1-1/2 inches apart to make diamond shape pieces. Add 1-cup water and pour over the top.

Bake: between 325-350 degrees for 1 hour

FRIED KUFTA

Use the same wheat mixture and filling as (Soup Kufta with Yogurt). Prepare balls the same way but flatten the roundness of the kufta by pressing gently between the palms. Fry in olive oil on each side until browned.

TOMATO OR GREEN PEPPER (DOLMA)

Mixture:
2 cups bulgur wheat (medium ground).
1-1/3 lb. lean ground beef
3 to 4 Tbs. thick tomato paste (homemade is best).
1 large onion (chopped fine).
Salt to taste

Combine all ingredients and mix well. Stuff tomato or green peppers. Line pan with extra tomatoes or green peppers to prevent burning. Then place dolma in alternating layers. Place plate and weight on top and cover with distilled water.

Cook:
50 to 60 minutes (when it comes to a boil turn down to medium heat).

Serves: 10 to 12 persons

If using:
Dried tomatoes or green peppers - soak in boiling water until they are soft before stuffing.
Fresh tomatoes or green peppers - clean out center and wash out before stuffing.

Do not to cook in an aluminum pan.

SARMA WITH CABBAGE

Mixture:
2 cups uncooked rice (regular long grain) rinse in cold
        water before using.
1-1/3 lb. lean ground beef
4 Tbs. thick tomato paste (homemade is best or use fresh
        tomatoes).
1/3 tsp. black pepper or 1/8 tsp. red pepper
1 medium onion (chopped fine)
1 medium green pepper (diced)
Salt to taste

Combine all ingredients and mix well. Put mixture on prepared cabbage leaf and loosely roll. Place sarma rolls in any kind of pan. Layer in alternating directions. **NOTE:** Line bottom of pan with extra cabbage leaves. Sprinkle with about 1 tsp. Salt and 2-3 tsp. dried crumbled mint. Place plate with weight (flat rock optional) on top. Cover with water.

Cook:
45 minutes (when water comes to a boil reduce heat to a little below medium).
Serves: 10 to 12 persons

How to Prepare Cabbage:
When buying cabbage get one that is loose, not solid. Cut out the core and separate the leaves. Cut the heavy part close to leaf off. Place leaves in large pan and pour boiling water over them. Let stand until they are wilted. Line your cooking pan with extra cabbage leaves.

SARMA WITH GRAPE LEAVES

Mixture:
2 cups bulgur wheat (medium ground)
1-1/3 lbs. Lean ground beef
3 to 4 Tbs. thick tomato paste (homemade is best)
1 small dried chili pepper or 1/3 tsp. Cayenne pepper
1/2 small onion (diced)
Salt to taste

Combine all ingredients and mix well. Put mixture on prepared grape leaf and loosely roll. Place sarma roll in porcelain pan in layers alternation directions. Line bottom of pan with extra grape leaves. Place plate and weight on top and cover with water. Put 1/3 tsp. tartaric acid or 1/8 tsp. Sumac paste.

Cook:
40 to 50 minutes (when boils turn down to medium heat).

Serves: 10 to 12 persons

How to Prepare Grape Leaves:
Pick large leaves. Wash and cut off stem. Place the leaves in a large pan and pour boiling water over them. Let them stand until wilted or until they change color. Line your cooking pan with extra grape leaves.

Do not to cook in an aluminum pan.

GLUTEN

3 cups cold water
7 cups whole-wheat flour

Mix water and flour. Knead well for 15-20 minutes.

To extract gluten from the kneaded dough. Put dough in a bowl and cover dough with water. Work dough by kneading it with your hands. Work dough under cold tap water until water runs clear under the dough. The dough will feel like bubble gum. Be careful not to wash all of the bran out.

Bake in greased loaf pan with beef or chicken broth covering about 1/2 inch above gluten. Bake at 300 degrees for 2 to 4 hours (until gluten has firm texture) should spring back to touch and broth will be nearly gone. Remove from oven and slice it into steaks.

OAT- VEGGIE BURGERS

3-1/2 cups water
1/2 cup hulled sunflower seeds (ground)
1 large onion (chopped)
4 bouillon cubes
4-1/2 cups rolled oats
1 large green pepper (chopped)
1 clove garlic (minced)
1/2 cup carrots (finely grated)
1 Tbs. Italian Seasoning

Place all of the ingredients, except for the oats, in a large saucepan and bring to a boil. Turn off heat. Add oats and mix until well combined. Press down the mixture in the pan and let it set for about 15 minutes. Then scoop the mixture into heaping 1/2 cups and place rounded mixture on a lightly greased cookie sheet. Press mixture into a burger shape with a fork.

Bake at 400 degrees. For 25 minutes on the 1st side.

Bake for 20 minutes on the 2nd side on the bottom rack of the oven.

FALYNN'S
CRYSTALINE COOKIES

2 cups soft white wheat flour
3/4 cup natural applesauce (lower in sugar).
1/4 cup honey
1/4 tsp. salt
1/2 tsp. baking soda
2 handfuls of chocolate chips (Crystaline Chocolate preferred).

Mix all wet ingredients first. Then, add dry ingredients.

Stir until moist. Add chocolate chips. Drop spoon size amounts onto non-stick cookie sheet.

Bake at 350 degrees for 10-11 minutes.

Best served while warm!

UNLEAVENED BREAD

2-1/2 cup whole-wheat flour
1/3 cup olive oil
1/2 tsp. salt
1 cup distilled water

Sift flour into bowl with salt. Add oil slowly while mixing. Add water and mix well, until smooth. If sticky add a little more flour but not too much.

Shape into biscuits, small and flat.

Bake in preheated oven 375 degrees about 10 minutes, then reduce heat to 275 degrees and bake an additional 30 minutes or until baked through.

UNLEAVENED BREAD STICKS

2 cups sifted whole wheat flour *or* Spelt

OR

1 cup soft pastry white flour (ground from your white wheat)
1/4 cup oat flour (ground from oat groats)
1/2 cup whole wheat flour *or* spelt

Add:
1 Tbs. Sugar or equivalent
1/2 tsp. salt
3 Tbs. Olive oil
3/4 cup cold distilled water

Knead about 7 minutes.

Roll into pencil-like strips about 8 inches long and 1/2 inch wide. Place on a greased sheet pan.

Bake at 350 degrees for 1/2 hour or until golden brown.

SISTER GEORGE'S WHOLE WHEAT BREAD

2/3-cup oil
2/3-cup honey
2-1/2 Tbs. Yeast
14 cups flour (whole wheat)
6 cups warm water
2 Tbs. salt

Mix oil, honey, yeast, 6 cups flour, and water. Mix for 3 minutes and rest for 8 minutes.

Add: 2 Tbs. Salt & enough flour till it is not sticky, which will be 6-8 cups whole-wheat flour.

Knead 5 minutes on high speed. Then let rest for 10 minutes.

Shape into six (6) one (1) lb. loaves (Smaller pans).

Let rise about 30 minutes.

Bake 40-45 minutes at 350 degrees.

EZEKIEL BREAD

3-1/2 cups wheat
3-1/2 cups spelt
1-cup barley
1/4 cup pinto beans
1/4 cup soybeans
1/4 cup lentils
1 cup rye
1/3 cup millet
5 cups warm water

1/2 cup olive oil
1/2 cup molasses
1/2 cup honey
3 Tbs. Yeast
2 Tbs. Salt
1/2 cup gluten four
2 Tbs. Dough enhancer
6 Tbs. Lecithin
1/4 tsp. baking soda

Combine the 5 cups warms water, honey, and yeast, set aside and let it brew about 10-15 minutes. Combine the grains and beans and grind into flour and set aside. Combine the remaining ingredients. Add 1/2 of the flour and mix together. Add the water, honey, and yeast mixture. Add more of the flour until dough pulls away from the sides of the bowl. Then knead 6-8 minutes. Shape into loaves and let rise until double in size.

Bake at 350 degrees for 35 minutes. Makes 4 loaves.

EZEKIEL FLOUR

Ezekiel 4:9

Take thou also unto thee wheat, and barley, and beans, and lentils, and millet, and fitches (Spelt), and put them in one vessel, and make thee bread thereof.....

10 cups or parts wheat
 1 cup or part barley
 1 cup or part beans (any kind or combination).
 1 cup or part lentils (green or red).
 1 cup or part millet
10 cups or parts spelt, or hard white wheat, or rye, or a combination of all three grains. This is in addition to the above wheat.

If you don't have spelt you can substitute hard white wheat or rye.

Mix together and grind to fine flour just before using.

Freeze any remaining flour for future use.

GRAINS FOR BABIES

One part Oat Groats
One part Hulled Barley
One part Brown Rice
One part Hulled Millet

Mix these grains together, and grind very fine.

Freeze un-used grain.

Baby Food

1 Tbs. Grain mixture
1/2 cup cold Distilled Water
Banana or apple sauce optional

Mix the grain and cold water
Cook stirring with a wire whip until it comes to a boil.
Remove from heat.
Cool until just warm
Add the fruit

This recipe is also good for people who are just starting to use whole grains, and for people who have digestive problems. After using this mix for a while, the next grain that should be added is hulled buckwheat.

A BASIC GRAIN MIX

One to Five parts Wheat (soft or hard)
One part Oat Groats
One part Hulled Barley
One part Brown Rice
One part Hulled Millet
One part whole Rye
One part Corn

Grind into flour

Freeze un-used flour.

Waffles and Pancakes

1/4 tsp. Baking Soda
1/2 tsp. Salt
1 cup Distilled Water
1 cup Grain Flour Mixture
1/8 cup Olive Oil
1 Egg

Mix together add additional flour mixture to thicken for waffles. Add 1/4 tsp. baking powder for waffles.

BANNA'S BEANS

2 cups pinto beans
1 cup small red beans
1 Tbs. basil
1 Tbs. oregano
1 tomato
2 small potatoes
1 large red onion
2 garlic cloves

Soak beans overnight.
Drain beans.
Add more water back into the pan with the beans and bring to a boil.
Drain beans again and rinse thoroughly.
Add water back into the pan with the beans.
Add all ingredients
Cook beans and ingredients on medium to low heat for 2-3 hours.
Pour all into blender.
Blend until smooth (similar to refried beans).

Serve in taco shells or whatever sounds good!

PINTO BEAN FUDGE

2 lbs. Milk chocolate chips (5 ½ cups)
1 cube of butter
4 cups sugar
½ cup pinto bean flour
1 can evaporated milk
½ cup water
1 tsp. vanilla

Combine and set aside Chocolate chips and butter.

Mix sugar and bean flour well.
Combine with milk and water.
Boil for 7 minutes stirring constantly.
Pour hot sugar and milk mixture over chips and butter.
Stir until melted.
Add vanilla.
Pour into buttered 13 x 17 pan and put into the refrigerator to set up.

Suggested books for Recipes

Allergy Cooking With Ease, Nicolette Drumke gives many recipes that use stevia. You may want to try her carob cake and cookies if you have children who need healthier cakes. She warns that stevia-sweetened baked goods do not brown very much, so when baking, check them for doneness by touching and not by color.

The Body Ecology Diet, Donna Gates with Linda Schartz gives insight to the acid and alkaline conditions of our bodies and the knowledge of how to keep our bodies slightly alkaline for optimal health. They also provide recipes on using Millet, Quinoa, and Amaranth, along with understanding refined and unrefined oils and stevia. This book is based on relieving the condition of Candida (yeast over growth). Even if you do not have this condition, the foods listed in this book are very high in the nutrients our bodies so desperately need.

The Sprouting Book, Ann Wigmore This book was written for everyone who is interested in good nutrition at a low cost (and with great taste) this highly practical and fully illustrated book provides readers with all the information necessary to start and maintain an indoor sprout garden. The book discusses a variety of sprouts and sprouting methods, explains the sprouts' importance in a healthy diet, and presents a wealth of simple and delicious recipes.

Appendix

FOR MORE INFORMATION ON ORDERING:

Juicers
Wheatgrass Juicers
Soymilk Machines
Blenders
Grain Mills
Flax Seed Grinders
Dehydrators
Water Distillers
Yogurt Makers
Sprouters
Wheatgrass Growing Kit

WRITE TO:

A to Z Nutrition
658 Goldenwood Court
Powder Springs, GA 30127

1-888-889-2381
www.atoznutrition.org

Bibliography

American Institute for Cancer Research, 1984 88pg, Planning Meals that Lower Cancer Risk: A reference guide.

Claessens, Sharon, *Healthy Cooking,* (Emmaus, PA: Rodale Press, 1984)

Combs, Michael, *An Ounce of Prevention, A quick reference guide to Herbs, Vitamins, and Minerals,* The University of the Great Spirit of Healing.

Connor, Sonja L,RD and William E, MD, *The New American Diet* (New York: Simon & Schuster, 1986 410pg)

Gates, Donna with Linda Schatz, *The Body Ecology Diet, Recovering Your Health and Rebuilding Your Immunity,* Fourth Edition, B.E.D. Publications, Atlanta, Georgia, 1996.

Haas, Elson M, *Staying Healthy with Nutrition, The complete Guide to diet and Nutritional Medicine,* Celestial Arts Publication, Berkley California, 1992.

Page, Linda, *Healthy Healing,* Traditional Wisdom Inc., Eleventh Edition, Revised/Updated, March 2000.

The Merck Manual of Medical Information Home Edition, Pocket Books, 1997

Papadenenis,Wendy, *Cognizance,* Return to Eden publications, Essential Fatty Acids, Stevia, Enzymes.